A BOOK ABOUT CHILDREN

CHRISTIAN CHILDREN'S FUND
1938 - 1991

Larry E. Tise

Published and Distributed for the
Christian Children's Fund, Inc.

by

Hartland Publishing
Falls Church, Virginia

7-17-02

Library of Congress Cataloging-in-Publication Data

Tise, Larry E.
    A book about children : Christian Children's Fund 1938-1991 /
Larry E. Tise.
        p.   cm.
    Includes bibliographical references and index.
    ISBN 0-9634400-0-4 (alk. paper)
    1. Christian Children's Fund--History. I. Title.

HV703.C6T57 1992
362.7'1--dc20   92-34960
                                                    CIP

FOREWORD

"This is a book about children. In every country, among all peoples, children are the greatest national treasure, longed for and cherished by their families and communities. The instinct is sound, for children are the hope for human survival. When the natural environment of family and society is destroyed by war and catastrophe, and above all by war, the children are the ones who suffer most. Then the treasure is wasted and the loss to mankind is severe."

Pearl S. Buck
from the foreword *Children of Calamity* (1957)

It was with those gentle and caring words that beloved novelist Pearl S. Buck opened the foreword to the first history of Christian Children's Fund in 1957. In many ways her sentiments are still appropriate today in describing the single-minded focus of an organization that has evolved to become perhaps the world's most powerful global force in the interests of children: not only those who are distressed, but also those who live in intolerable conditions. To this day CCF is devoted to the welfare of children, their families *and* their communities wherever there is need.

But need is no longer seen as deriving primarily from the devastations of war. War is just one of the means whereby children are deprived of their essential rights to grow to adulthood in today's world. Economic deprivation, abject poverty, the absence of basic health care or even minimal educational opportunities—not to mention such other essentials as clean drinking water, sanitary sewage disposal, and a place to sleep—are other conditions that affect the majority of the world's children. And these are quite apart from those other tragic calamities—war, disease, famine, storm, and earthquake—so feared by Pearl Buck's generation.

And CCF is no longer merely an "adoption" agency operated personally and directly by a devoted, but perhaps isolated group of folk in Richmond, Virginia, with the generous support of a few thousand contributing "sponsors" around the United States. Whereas in 1957 CCF's principal means of assisting children was to house them in beautifully maintained orphanages and to give them the rudiments of education, today CCF assists children through projects designed to help the children's entire families and communities. While in 1957 CCF worked primarily on the western edge of the Pacific rim (in Taiwan, Korea, Japan, the Philippines, and India), CCF today operates on every continent in long-term community development projects. While in 1957 CCF was primarily focused on caring for and improving the lives of "sponsored" children, CCF today is prepared to intervene with financial, administrative, and policy support throughout the world.

Another substantial difference from 1957 is CCF's ability to deliver services. In 1957 CCF's income for the year was $3,577,755. Of that amount $2,619,707 was sent overseas to assist perhaps 30,000 children who were housed in some four hundred orphanages in more than forty countries. Much of this support was used to administer homes which were owned, operated, and maintained by CCF, such as the extensive Children's Garden in Hong Kong. Today, however, through dedicated work and the devoted generosity of sponsors, contributors, and other friends, CCF's revenues have increased by a hundred million dollars to the $103 million level. Of that amount $82.5 million is sent to assist some 533,000 children worldwide. But with the family and community focus of CCF's efforts today, these funds are leveraged in communitywide projects that positively affect the lives of many more hundreds of thousands of people. And given CCF's active and enthusiastic involvement in the "Rights of the Child" movement spearheaded by the United Nations and endorsed by most nations of the earth, the impact of CCF's work is sure to grow in the future.

CCF's story—both its illustrious past and its vibrant present—is nothing short of amazing, even inspiring. It is for that reason that I eagerly embraced the notion when I came to CCF in 1988 that its history should be told. I wanted to see the story researched, written, and fully presented for the instruction and appreciation of everyone associated with CCF— sponsors, friends and supporters, staff and field workers—and, yes, also for those who have been and are the principal beneficiaries of CCF's work—the children of the world. I am pleased to see the results contained in the pages that follow and commend them to you.

Dr. Paul F. McCleary, Executive Director
Christian Children's Fund, Inc.

TABLE OF CONTENTS

LIST OF ILLUSTRATIONS

PREFACE

A Rendezvous with the Past

When I received a call from Christian Children's Fund (CCF) during the summer of 1991 asking if I would be interested in editing and writing a history of its global efforts to assist children for over half a century, I could not resist the feeling that this was a rendezvous with the past. As I listened to a description of the undertaking, I could hardly restrain my enthusiasm. Fortunately I did, however, and heard that I was being contacted because of my reputation as a historian and as someone who had written about various aspects of American religious history. Moreover, I had been recommended as one who might be able to help CCF gather up its rather extensive archival materials and add some historical dimensions to an existing manuscript describing CCF's work around the world today.

There were a couple of things my CCF caller did not know. First, he did not know that I was—in addition to my doctoral training in history—also a divinity graduate and an ordained Methodist minister with a deep and abiding interest in America's fervent missionary movements around the world. Growing up in North Carolina during the 1950s in a tiny Methodist church, one could hardly avoid the frequent and moving appeals we all heard to help the less fortunate people of the world. Missionaries on furlough often came to our church and excited us with all of the needs and opportunities to assist people in every part of the globe.

The second thing my caller did not know about was CCF Adoption #27966 at Home #23. These numbers refer to one Young Kon who was described as a boy born May 7, 1951. It just so happens that Young Kon is none other than that CCF child from Korea who was "adopted" by my Sunday school class at Mt. Tabor Methodist Church in Winston-Salem, North Carolina, sometime around 1956 or 1957. Somehow I had ended up being the class coordinator for this project and principal contact both with CCF and with Young Kon. It was, without a doubt, one of those formative and memorable experiences of my teenage years that sensitized me to the important work done by CCF around the world.

My years of close involvement spanned the era when CCF's

principal means of assisting children was through orphanages and boarding schools. I distinctly recall the excitement of receiving news about CCF's work, of learning about the conditions of children in various countries and cultures, and of getting letters from our "adopted" child. One of the highlights of these years was the receipt of a copy of Edmund W. Janss' little paperback book titled *Yankee Si! The Story of Dr. J. Calvitt Clarke and His 36,000 Children*. I read the book from cover to cover, savoring the inspiring story of Dr. Clarke and the devoted band of CCF workers around the world.

Although our Sunday school class eventually drifted away from the sponsorship, a permanent mark had been made that sensitized me for life to the workings of CCF and other child assistance organizations. Though I did not follow it intimately, my heart was always warmed whenever I saw reference to CCF, noticed its television and magazine appeals, or heard about its inspired interventions to assist distressed children. In a special way, I mentally chronicled its manifestations as an interested observer for a period of nearly thirty years.

When I happily agreed to assist with the project, therefore, it was like filling in the pieces of a somewhat familiar puzzle. I found the previous histories of CCF, one by John C. Caldwell in 1957 and the one by Edmund W. Janss, to be most helpful. I also pored through the published reports and the executive minutes of CCF from the beginning. I spent a number of good hours at CCF talking with some of the folk who have been with the organization for many years, especially Jim Hostetler, Betty Davidson, and former CCF public relations manager Don Murray. On other visits I was able to meet some of CCF's impassioned and dedicated national directors. They are both a pleasure and an inspiration to know.

But the principal source for much of what appears in the following pages was collected by journalist Kristin Helmore, formerly of *The Christian Science Monitor* and now editor of *African Farmer* for The Hunger Project, as she traveled about the world visiting CCF project sites on three continents and in numerous countries. Helmore is a prolific and well-known writer on Third World development concerns. From 1985 until 1989 she was Third World correspondent for *The Christian Science Monitor*. There she prepared major series of articles on women in the developing world, the exploitation of children around the world, community development programs in Third World nations, and the life of poor blacks in America. These stories garnered her a variety of prestigious journalism awards.

In 1989 and 1990 she spent several months visiting CCF projects in Kenya, Ethiopia, Sierra Leone, Brazil, Guatemala, the Philippines, Indonesia, and India. As background for her visits, she culled through

CCF files in Richmond and in various CCF national offices so that she could portray CCF at work assisting children, their families and communities from the ground up around the world. Her on-site profiles of CCF project communities will appear in a companion volume to this history to be published by CCF in the near future. Her background files, stories, and notes provide much of the grist that eventually went into the history presented here.

I am grateful for the opportunity of telling CCF's compelling story. And I am grateful for assistance specifically rendered over the past months by William R. Dixon, Director of Development for CCF, and by Cheri Dahl, CCF Public Relations Manager. Also of assistance have been CCF's regional coordinators who read the pertinent parts of the manuscript for accuracy: James Hostetler, Eastern Europe; Sarah Manning, Asia; Anthony Ramos, Latin America; Joyce Dougan, Africa; and Thomas Rhodenbaugh, U.S. and Caribbean. CCF national directors and the directors of CCF's international partnership organizations also reviewed sections on their own nations. The most valuable editorial assistants, however, were Dr. Paul McCleary himself and Joan Losen of CCF's Development Office. Both of them have gifted and keen eyes for clear expression, precise meaning, and correct detail. And, of course, without the encouragement and support of Dr. McCleary in his role as Executive Director of CCF, the project would never have gotten off the ground.

I have also received invaluable encouragement and support in this project during these months from colleagues and from my associates at The Franklin Institute. I hereby express my heartfelt appreciation to especially Vivian W. Piasecki, Ann V. Satterthwaite, Nancy D. Kolb, Kathleen Fau, Berrie Torgan, and Paul Leach.

As a historian—as well as a longtime observer of CCF—I am happy to share this story with both CCF friends and others who are interested in the history of global efforts to assist children. There is much herein about American philanthropy but also about the changing ways in which that charitable spirit has been expressed over time. No one would think today of creating a CCF the way it did business in its earliest days. But without those early trials and experiments, those valiant efforts to save children in the most alarming of circumstances, we would not have today a mature and effective Christian Children's Fund—truly a global force for children.

Larry E. Tise, Ph.D., Executive Director
Benjamin Franklin National Memorial
The Franklin Institute
Philadelphia, Pennsylvania

A Book

About Children

Chapter One

CREATION OF CHINA'S CHILDREN FUND, 1938-1946

Richmond, Virginia—1938

J. Calvitt Clarke, Presbyterian minister, veteran promoter of relief for peoples displaced by the ravages of the First World War, and a gifted publicist and fundraiser, was on his way from New York to Chambersburg, Pennsylvania, in late summer of 1938. On the train he ran into a friend, Dr. J. Stewart Nagle, a former Methodist missionary with years of experience in the Far East. Nagle was founder of a school in Singapore for Chinese boys orphaned as a result of the Japanese aggression against China.

As the train clicked noisily down the tracks, and warm air and soot poured in through the open windows, the two friends found themselves discussing a subject that had been preying on both their minds in recent weeks: the news of atrocities, famine, bombings, and the suffering of tens of thousands of civilians—particularly children—in the wake of the Japanese invasion of China. It would later be estimated that between one and two million Chinese children died between 1937 and 1940 alone.

Horrors like these, and the yearning to do something about them, were nothing new to Clarke. Since his college days before World War I, he had organized committees in support of Near East Relief, an agency that sent food and clothing to war-torn Armenia and Syria. In the early 1920s, he had joined that organization and traveled to Mt. Ararat and Palestine, witnessing firsthand the suffering of war and famine victims. Time and again, what affected him most was the children.

3

By 1932, the bleakest year of the Depression in the United States, Clarke again turned his concern for children in need into action. With Dr. Nagle and another colleague, Dr. John Voris, he co-founded a unique new organization, Save the Children Federation, to aid children in Harlan County, Kentucky, one of the most impoverished regions of the country. He served as southern director of Save the Children, from his home base in Richmond, Virginia, until 1937. Since that time, Save the Children evolved into one of the world's well-known international child sponsorship agencies, similar in many ways to the institution Clarke was momentarily to bring to life—Christian Children's Fund.[1]

The train pulled into Chambersburg, and the two men went their separate ways. But as he walked the shady streets of the quiet little town, Clarke could not get one question out of his mind. It stayed with him as he conducted his business, and was still nagging at him when he ran right into the very person who might help him answer it. As Clarke passed a barbershop, there was his friend Nagle once again, heading down the sidewalk toward him.

It seems that Nagle had not been able to shake their earlier conversation either.

"You know, Champ," said Nagle, using a nickname Clarke had acquired in college. "I've been thinking about our conversation on the train this morning—about what's going on in China."

So had Clarke. Without hesitation, he asked the question that had been gnawing at him. "Do you feel that Americans are doing all they can to help?"

There was a pause, and then Nagle lifted one eyebrow and smiled. "You're a good fundraiser, why don't *you* do something about it?"

Clarke didn't answer right away. He stood there, staring into the window of the barbershop. What he saw was his own reflection, staring back at him: nothing extraordinary or particularly impressive, nothing to suggest the man of vision and dedication whose work would eventually improve the lives of millions of children and their families all over the world—just a tallish, balding man of 51 in a loose-fitting suit, slightly stooped, with a long nose and a rather shy expression.

"All right," he said quietly, glancing back at his friend. "I will."

Clarke returned to his home in Richmond, and with his wife's help

---

[1] The dramatic story of the creation of China's Children Fund and what was to become Christian Children's Fund is told in a variety of places including John C. Caldwell, *Children of Calamity* (New York: John Day Company, 1957), pp. 30-33; Edmund W. Janss, *Yankee Si! The Story of Dr. J. Calvitt Clarke and His 36,000 Children* (New York: William Morrow & Company, 1961), pp. 27- 38 (paper edition); and Edmund W. Janss, *A Brief History of Christian Children's Fund, Inc.* (typescript; revised, 1967), pp. 1-15.

he launched a nationwide appeal for funds in behalf of China's children, working out of his home and spending his own money for stationery and postage. Nagle was right: the shy Presbyterian had a knack for raising money, for convincing people, even during the Depression, to share with children on the other side of the world who were in desperate need. He'd been honing this talent since the 1920s when, among other things, he organized the largest-ever collection of used clothing in behalf of Armenian and Syrian refugees.

Now, in 1938, with the suffering of China's children heavy on his heart, Clarke set in motion a deceptively simple fundraising strategy that was to prove immensely successful for more than 50 years. By 1991 his scheme would produce more than $100 million annually in support of suffering children throughout the world. And also in that year his creature—Christian Children's Fund—would pass the $1 billion mark in funds transmitted from the United States to other nations caring for homeless children, assisting families in distress, and in building up entire communities in poverty-stricken areas so that the children of the world might not only survive, but also find meaningful places in their own societies.

Clarke's "secret weapon" was individual, person-to-person child sponsorship (originally called "adoption")—no government funds, no ideological agendas, a minimum amount of bureaucracy—just individual people who cared about others and were willing to send small amounts of money on a regular basis to help an individual child in need. This individual-help system and a direct sponsor-to-child relationship, would eventually expand to encompass the child's entire family and community.

But the essential fact for Clarke was that the children he was helping were war orphans; they had been cut adrift from their families and communities. Hence, an institution that could supply the food, shelter and education formerly provided by the children's families was what was first needed.

Once Clarke made up his mind to take the initiative, things moved like a whirlwind. Between his August trip to Chambersburg and February 1939—a mere six months later—he had launched an organization and was already sending money to save the starving children of China. On October 6 he went before the State Corporation Commission of Virginia and got a charter for what he decided to call China's Children Fund, Incorporated. Just two months later, on December 9, he convened the first meeting of this novel Fund in "a private dining room at the Occidental Restaurant, 212 N. Eighth Street" in Richmond. This Occidental Restaurant would serve well as the meeting place of CCF's Board of Directors for years to come. When the Board next met on

February 21, 1939, there were already 450 members of CCF's "National Committee" and the Board had sufficient funds raised to send CCF's first contribution, $2,000, "to the authorities in China."[2]

From the first it was clear that CCF was a creation of, and would be a monument to the energy and ingenuity of, Calvitt Clarke. At the first meeting—with only Clarke's promise of funds that would be forthcoming—commitments against the future were made. Clarke had already opened offices for the Fund in the Richmond Trust Building on Main Street in Richmond. And he persuaded the Board to start him out on a salary of $50 a week beginning in January 1939.

Urging him on at that first meeting was a distinguished group of Virginians headed by Eudora Ramsay Richardson and T. Nelson Parker. Mrs. Richardson, a factor in Richmond culture and society, was elected the first president of CCF. Parker, a former mayor of Richmond and Commissioner of Insurance for the Commonwealth of Virginia, was elected the first secretary. These were important selections since Mrs. Richardson would remain at the helm until 1944, when Parker would succeed her and continue as president for nearly 30 years. Underscoring an amazing continuity of leadership through the history of CCF is the fact that Mrs. Richardson's place on the CCF executive committee was taken by Verbon E. Kemp, Executive Director of the Virginia State Chamber of Commerce from 1935 until 1963, who then succeeded Clarke as only the second Executive Director of CCF.[3]

From the second meeting of the board when Clarke recommended an intitial contribution of $2,000 to China relief, the growth of CCF was nothing short of phenomenal. Just twelve months after the organizational meeting, he reported that a total of $13,000 had been sent to the KuKong Orphanage headed by J. R. Saunders and to Ling Nan University. Other funds were sent directly to Madame Chiang Kai-shek—a great heroine to Americans—"for the children she is caring for." Two days after the Japanese attacked Pearl Harbor, CCF authorized $25,000 to be sent to areas of China not occupied by Japanese, as the U.S. government would allow. By the midpoint of the Second World War, CCF was sending $65,000 every six months. The amount sent in fiscal year 1943-44 was $186,726. And in the last year of the war, fiscal year 1945-46, the amazing sum of $372,217 was sent by CCF to China.[4]

---

[2] CCF Executive Committee Minutes, December 9, 1938, and February 21, 1939.

[3] CCF Executive Committee Minutes, November 8, 1944. Janss, *Brief History*, pp. 159, 162.

[4] CCF Executive Committee Minutes, December 27, 1939; December 11, 1940; December 9, 1941; April 20, 1943; January 27, 1944. For the CCF Summary of Receipts & Expenditures for 1938 through 1991, see Appendix 1.

In a period of little more than six years Clarke and his Richmond colleagues and supporters had wrought a minor miracle and had become a force to reckon with. The secret to the miracle was CCF's very popular "adoption" plan developed sometime prior to 1941. According to this plan, individual donors could contribute a set amount of money per month and per year and "adopt" an orphaned child in China. As of July 31, 1941, Clarke told his board that this plan was working very well and that the current rate of $24 per child per year should be continued even though it "is now costing more than $24 per year to take care of these orphans." He thought it "was a good idea not to ask the sponsors of each child to pay any more at the present time unless they so desired." This notation in CCF's board minutes documents that CCF was the earliest of the various international child assistance organizations to employ this form of "adoption" as a mechanism for raising funds.[5]

The popularity of CCF's approach to connecting donors with a specific child gave the incipient Fund sufficient muscle that it could counter retrogressive national policies. By late 1942 CCF was invited to participate in the United China Relief Program of the War Relief Control Board of the U.S. government. CCF members prayed over this invitation extendedly and came to the conclusion that CCF should not belong. This was not due to exclusivity. It was rather that CCF's leaders concluded they could raise much more money on their own to assist children in China than would be possible if they were under the wing of a government bureau. Under tremendous pressure from federal officials, CCF reluctantly joined the United China Relief Program in December 1942. When annual revenues remained stagnant in the following year, however, CCF withdrew in protest from the program.[6]

Throughout the Second World War CCF's fortunes continued to grow. By November 1944 the organization was assisting 45 orphanages throughout China. When the war ended in 1945, indeed, CCF's income greatly exceeded the known needs in China. As a consequence, the board began looking to much larger horizons. As early as February 1946, funds were being sent to orphanages in the Philippines and Burma. Only a year later operations were being expanded into Japan, Korea, and other realms of the Asian continent. With each new commitment it became increasingly clear that Calvitt Clarke's idea of a privately funded assistance program for suffering children was here to stay.[7]

---

[5] CCF Executive Committee Minutes, July 31, 1941.

[6] CCF Executive Committee Minutes, December 29, 1942; June 18, 1943; October 10, 1944.

[7] CCF Executive Committee Minutes, November 8, 1944; February 7, 1946; November 19, 1946.

Things were looking so promising, in fact, that Clarke made something of a triumphal tour of 21 of the orphanages being assisted by CCF in China in the spring of 1946. Between May 31 and July 15 Clarke went to the six CCF orphanages in Peking; four in Hong Kong; two in Shanghai; and a raft of others in the bustling city of Canton. He was unable to visit others in Changtu, Kunming, Chungking, or to Shiu Chow—site of KuKong Orphanage headed by J. R. Saunders, the first home assisted by CCF. He nevertheless met with Saunders and representatives of all the orphanages assisted while he traveled around Canton. He also reviewed CCF's increasingly complex overseas operations with the Rev. Erwin W. Raetz who had been appointed in 1943 to coordinate the organization's assistance programs in China.[8]

Everywhere he went, Clarke was treated with honor and glory. He made endless addresses, was feted at luncheons and dinners, and entertained by children at each of CCF's orphanages. He was "greatly impressed with the cooperation and appreciation of the Chinese, with the fine reputation our organization has built up for itself in China, with the confidence and appreciation for our work held by government officials, welfare workers not connected with China's Children Fund, Mission Board secretaries and various business men and women. China's Children Fund is well known in China and accepted as an important and efficient welfare organization."

Satisfied that things were well in hand in China, Clarke paused along the way to meet with the folk who would shortly open up CCF's operations in Burma.[9] There seemed to be no reason not to expand throughout Asia.

~~~

Canton, China—1946

The children called it "The Big Wash."

Not since they moved into this abandoned high school in Canton's Honam district the year before had the place undergone such an overhaul. The school had been built by the Japanese for the children of "puppet" soldiers—those who collaborated with the Japanese during

---

[8] Dr. J. R. Saunders of the KuKong Orphanage had been designated "our representative in China" on August 6, 1942, but he was replaced by Raetz in 1943. The various approaches to CCF's role in China appear in the minutes of the executive committee. CCF Executive Committee Minutes, August 6, 1942; November 8, 26, 1943; January 27, 1944. J. Calvitt Clarke, Report of Survey in China, May 31-July 15, 1946.

[9] Clarke, Report of Survey in China, pp. 1, 4.

their occupation of Canton and other Chinese coastal cities. In 1945, after the war was over, 700 children, ranging in age from five to 14, were brought here down the Pearl River from makeshift orphanages in Toishan, in the famine-ridden Sz Yup (pronounced see-up) delta to the South.

Boys outnumbered girls by two to one—an anomaly with a horrifying history. When famine struck their native, low-lying, densely populated region, many parents had sold their daughters to wealthy families in order to buy food. The tiny slaves received no education, and were often mistreated, abused, and neglected. Undoubtedly, many starved, since in Sz Yup the famine was so severe that even the well-to-do were dying of hunger. A substantial percentage of the 700 orphans, in fact, were from middle-class families who had starved to death along with the poor.

When they arrived in Canton in late 1945, the children found the abandoned high school deserted, neglected, and filthy. Grass growing wild in the courtyard was taller than they were—perfect for hide-and-seek. Yet even the little ones understood that untended grass in their beautiful, impressive new home was not quite right. The large glass windows, designed to let in floods of light, were blackened with grime; dust and dirt were everywhere, and there was no furniture in the classrooms, dormitories, or dining room.

"The kids thought it was great," the Reverend Verent J. Mills, director of the orphanage, recalled some 44 years later. Indeed, the children were so excited at being moved to this large dwelling with its promise of light-filled rooms, electricity and dependable supplies of food, that they immediately threw themselves into the task of setting things right. It was the children who cut the grass, cleaned the windows, and scrubbed the floors, hauling up water in buckets from the nearby river. Dr. Mills arranged for the fabrication of simple wooden bunk beds, desks, and chairs. During the months before these were delivered, the children slept, ate, and studied on the floor. But their "nest-building" zeal and their cleaning and polishing, even before the furniture arrived, made the school the most comfortable home many of them had ever known.

And all this was just a warm-up for The Big Wash.

When Mills found these children a few years before, every one of them was near death from starvation. Most had watched their parents, sisters, and brothers die of hunger. Their home province, Kwangtung, with its long shoreline on the South China coast, is cut off from the rest of the country by a range of towering, jagged, fingerlike mountains— the very mountains that look so mysterious and improbable in Chinese paintings. The most densely populated region of China apart from the

Yangtze Valley, Kwangtung and its watery delta of Sz Yup have been for centuries totally dependent on imports of rice from Indochina (today Vietnam and Thailand) to the west and south. But with Japan's gradual blockade of the Chinese coast starting in 1937, and its invasion of Indochina in 1940, Kwangtung and the Sz Yup were eventually cut off from all supplies of food.

Mills had been the American Advisory Committee's field supervisor of famine relief in the unoccupied region of Sz Yup since 1941. In his work, he came across hundreds of children—sometimes alone, more often in small groups—wandering the countryside or haunting the villages of the delta. The British-born, Canadian-reared missionary had lived among the impoverished rural Chinese since 1931, but he had never seen suffering like this. The children he encountered reminded him of "packs of little wolves," searching, scavenging, begging for something to eat. When he took them in, setting up five improvised orphanages in the Sz Yup town of Toishan, all the children were malnourished, many with bloated stomachs and skeletal frames characteristic of progressive starvation. Some were covered with the spreading, open sores of scurvy.

Mills recounts how, in 1943, he came across the youngest of the 700 children who eventually moved with him to the converted high school in Canton after the war:

"I had to go down to Kwanghoi on the coast, just south of Macao, to see one of our big soup kitchens," he recalls. "At the time we were feeding the hungry people out in that area. I was with Mr. Lai How Ming, one of the men in my office in Toishan, who was helping me take care of the orphaned children we had taken in. We left at about six in the morning, because we had quite a long way to walk. On the outskirts of Toishan city, right opposite the girls' normal school, there was a big cluster of bamboo. And right beside the road was a little boy. He looked more like a monkey than a human being—thin, drawn, the skin on his face parched and wrinkled. The child was starving to death. He couldn't stand up, he couldn't cry, he just made moaning sounds. He was probably two and a half or three, and there he was, sitting in his own mess, too weak to move.

"We went on our way—we couldn't stop. He was only one: everywhere you went, people were dying, starving—children starving everywhere. We went to Kwanghoi, and on our way back, as we came past the normal school, that little boy was still there. I thought to myself, 'He's too far gone to do anything without medical facilities.'

"We'd gone a considerable distance, and Mr. Lai turned to me and said, 'Pastor, I can't leave that little boy we passed back there. I'll never be able to sleep tonight if I don't go back and get him.' I said, 'How

Dr. Verent Mills in 1942 with some of the 142 starving children he rescued from Toishan, China

Ming, if you want to get him, we'll go back and get him.' So we went back, and I said, 'I'll carry him back to the home. He's filthy dirty, so I'll take some of these bamboo leaves on the ground, these big, long bamboo leaves, and I'll put them on my hand. And you take your two fingers and stick them under his armpits, and lift him up, and put him on the leaves in my hand.' Which he did. And when he put him on my hand, here was this little monkey face looking me right in the eye, and he smiled a monkey smile. Too weak to say anything, but he smiled thank you. When I think of it now, it just about rips the heart out of me—and I was going to pass that little boy by.

"So we took him to Number Two Home, and I told the ladies there to get some hot water and give him a bath and wash him up and get some clean clothes to put on him. And I told the cook to get some kongee, very thin kongee—kongee is rice gruel, a rice soup. I said, 'Only bring one bowl, no more.' So after he was washed, and they'd given him some tea to drink, he was getting his voice back, and he was starting to cry and holler. So they brought the kongee with this Chinese spoon. And when this child saw it, he just about went crazy—just ravenous. He went to grab the bowl and the spoon, wanted to put the whole thing in his mouth at once. So we had to hold his arms and feed him a spoonful at a time. And he'd no sooner get the spoon in his mouth than he'd start crying again, he was just so ravenous. So I said to the lady helping him, 'Take your time, don't be in a hurry. If you hurry, you'll kill him.'

"So—slowly—we fed him. When he finished the bowl he still wanted more. And by this time, the child had regained enough strength that he could really howl. He howled and howled. And I said, 'You can't give him anything more now for an hour.' It would have killed him. He'd been days without any fluid.

"Well, that little guy survived. We didn't know his name—he didn't even know his own name. If he wanted water, he could say 'water.' If he wanted rice, he could say 'rice.' But he didn't know his name, didn't know where his mommy and daddy were or anything. Probably his mother just left him there by the roadside, because she probably didn't have anything to eat either.

"This little guy began to put on weight, and I gave him a name, Lo Duk—it means 'Begotten of the Road.' But he had to have a surname, so Lai How Ming said, 'Well, he'll have to take your name, because you're the one that picked him up.' So they gave him my surname, Mei for Mills. So his name is Mei Lo Duk.

"After we got the kids from the five orphanages and moved them to Canton, here were 700 kids and he was the smallest one. He just about ran the outfit. He was spoiled rotten. If he fell down or anything and started to cry, the other children would come running like a swarm of bees to pick him up."

During the war years, Mills managed to arrange shelter for the children he rescued, but feeding them was far more difficult. He appealed to the foreign relief agencies based in China's wartime capital of Chungking, far to the northwest in Szechwan province. Before long, a number of donors, among them the Australian legation and the Canadian Red Cross, had sent him enough money to buy rice for the children.

Ironically, it was the ending of the war that put the children in danger of starvation again. When in August 1945, the Japanese surrendered, the relief agencies pulled out of Chungking, thinking that their work was done. Dr. Mills soon learned that he would have to find another source of funds to support the children. His response to the crisis was characteristic: he asked his 700 charges to help him pray.

"I told the kids they'd better pray the Lord would find another source of supply for us," he says. "If not, it would only be a matter of about three weeks when our rice would be used up, and we'd all have to go back on the street as beggars again."

The children prayed, but prayer had to be accompanied by action. Mills set out for Canton—about four days' journey from Toishan at a time when there were virtually no roads in the district. Arriving on a Sunday, he went to church. The speaker at the International Church in the International Settlement was a certain Reverend Erwin Raetz of the Dutch Reformed Church, from Grand Rapids, Michigan. While greeting the congregation after the service, Raetz asked Mills what had brought him to Canton. "When I told him what I was doing," Mills remembers, "he said, 'That's quite a coincidence. I've come back to China representing China's Children Fund of Richmond, Virginia. I suggest that you write to Dr. J. Calvitt Clarke and ask him to help you.'"

As a contract chaplain for the American Advisory Committee, Mills had special mail privileges which enabled him to dispatch a letter to Clarke in Richmond with unusual speed. He remained in Canton for the next two weeks awaiting a reply. At last, he says, "I received a cable from Dr. Clarke. He was taking us on, lock, stock, and barrel—700 children. To us it was a direct answer from heaven."

"Taking us on" meant that before long, regular payments corresponding to $2 per month per child began to arrive at the Bank of China in Toishan from Richmond, Virginia. In China in those days, the $2 a month for each child was sufficient to purchase adequate supplies of rice for all the children in Mills' care. But it had to be transported by rail from Hunan province, then carried by coolies on a five and a half day journey over the mountains and down the waterways and footpaths of Sz Yup to Toishan.

Mills soon concluded that the best way to secure a regular supply of food for his children was to move them—all 700, from five different homes—to Canton. Fortunately, Mills had friends in high places. Several years earlier, General Chiang Kai-shek himself had given Mills a personal introduction to the commander of the Southeast War Zone, General Cheung Fat Foi. General Cheung had made military shipments of rice available for Mills' earlier famine relief operations, and the two men had become friends. Now, General Cheung was stationed in Canton.

Mills visited the general and explained what he was looking for— a home for 700 children. Cheung's reply was immediate: "I think I've got just the property you need." The general summoned an aide, ordered a jeep, and Mills was immediately taken to Canton's Honam district on the other side of the Pearl River. There behind a high wall was the confiscated Japanese school: classrooms, dormitories, dining hall, kitchen and adjoining playing fields. Mills knew this was his answer. There remained only the challenge of transporting the 700 children from Toishan to Canton.

Once again, General Cheung stepped in. With his intervention, it was arranged that in ten days' time, the South China Steamship and Navigation Company would send two ships to the deep water town of Sam Fau. If Mills could get the children to Sam Fau, they would be taken by ship the rest of the way to Canton.

On the appointed day, when the two ships arrived in Sam Fau, Mills and his children were already on the dock waiting for them. "The ship's crew fed the children all the way to Canton," he says. "Those little kids thought they were in heaven."

Once installed in their new home, Mills and the children began to receive aid from other sources in addition to China's Children Fund. One such source, the United Nations Relief and Rehabilitation Administration, UNRRA, donated enough rice to fill two classrooms.[10] Mills' new orphanage also received bolts of surplus khaki fabric from the Chinese military, and soon the boys were wearing khaki shorts and shirts and the girls khaki skirts and blouses. Mosquito netting arrived—an essential item in Canton's hot, wet climate. And finally canned goods, along with bacon, butter, cheese, and fruit, came from the Philippines. At last, thought Mills, he could provide a balanced diet

---

[10] When UNRRA was disbanded in late 1946, its activities were divided among the various agencies of the fledgling United Nations. The needs of children for food, shelter, health care and education, which private organizations including CCF had already been addressing and championing in the international arena for a number of years, would become the global focus of the United Nations International Children's Emergency Fund (now officially the United Nations Children's Fund), better known as UNICEF.

for children who had eaten almost nothing but rice for years.

The children's immediate needs were taken care of. They were well fed and well housed, they attended school, and they even played volleyball, basketball, and their favorite game, ping-pong. In fact, they were scarcely recognizable as the skeletal, scavenging waifs they had been. But Mills was still worried about them. Their future was very uncertain, especially because they were orphans.

"In China an orphan was automatically assumed to be a thief and a liar," he explained. With no family ties to establish their identity, and no family members to vouch for their character, orphans were often outcasts, barely surviving on the margins of society. Mills couldn't let that happen to his children.

As the months went by, Mills continued to worry about the children and their future. Eventually, he devised a plan: He would teach them, in the most practical terms, how to provide for themselves, and how to be independent and self-reliant. He would see to it that every child learned a trade. And because he had been squirreling away some of his UNRRA funds against future needs, he had the resources in hand to establish a vocational training program at the home.

Mills himself had an unusual background for a missionary. His father was a metallurgist with the Canadian National Railways in Winnipeg, and he wanted—indeed, expected—his son to follow in his footsteps. Verent was sent to St. John's Technical High School to study engineering diesel technology. The plan was that father and son would someday work together. Instead, two missionaries from South China came to speak at the Millses' church on four successive evenings in 1931. At the conclusion of their last talk, 19-year-old Verent stepped forward to sign up as a missionary. When he left for China shortly thereafter, he was too young to be admitted to the Mission Board, was not ordained, and had never attended a seminary. What he did have, in addition to a wholehearted religious vocation, was a solid grounding in engineering and a talent for mechanics that, as it turned out, was to be invaluable in the years to come.

He was eminently qualified, for example, to go on a shopping expedition to Hong Kong in 1946, in search of machinery on which his children would be taught valuable mechanical skills. Within a week, he returned to Canton with four lathes, two drill presses, two shapers, and a milling machine for the boys, and with 12 industrial hand looms for the girls.

The metalworking machinery was installed in one classroom from which the desks had been removed. Holes had to be drilled in the floor and cement poured in order to fasten the heavy equipment in place. Ten to 12 boys could work in the shop at one time. At first, Mills taught the boys himself; later he hired an experienced machinist. When the boys-in-training were not working in the shop, they would be cutting and filing metal and threading bolts. As part of their training, the boys restored a progression of old trucks Mills had managed to acquire, fabricating all the needed parts themselves. The boys started their training at age 14; eventually every boy in the home had been taught machinery operation and repair, and many acquired a command of basic mechanics. All looked forward to the course. "It was considered a privilege to participate," says Dr. Mills.

Meanwhile, in a nearby classroom, 12 girls would be weaving cotton fabric on their looms, under the instruction of a man who had worked for many years in a textile mill. The girls made all the towels and underwear for the school. But most important, they too were learning to be self-supporting.

Several months after the children arrived in Canton, they were told that an important visitor—Dr. J. Calvitt Clarke of China's Children Fund—was coming from America far across the ocean to see them.

That is when The Big Wash began.

Once more, the many windows of the large orphanage had to be cleaned and the floors scrubbed. The two-tiered bunk beds had to be made neat and tidy, and the grass bed mats had to be washed. All bedding was neatly folded and placed at the head of each bed. Between each pair of bunks was a tall dresser with four drawers: one for the clothes and belongings of each of the four children who slept in the adjacent beds. All the clothes had to be taken out, carefully refolded, and replaced in the drawers. The bathrooms had to be scoured. The towels hanging outside the shower rooms had to be washed and put back neatly on their pegs below each child's name. The dining room floors and tables had to be scrubbed. The cupboards where the rice bowls, chopsticks, and plates were kept had to be cleaned, and new paper laid on the shelves. The kitchen had to be repainted, and the screened cupboards where the food was stored had to be varnished. The legs of the cupboards stood in bowls of water to prevent ants from getting into the food: the bowls had to be removed, washed and refilled with clean water.

The boys' vocational training workshop, with its lathes, drill presses, shapers, and milling machine had to be swept and scrubbed, and the machines cleaned and polished. The girls' looms had to be spotless, with no stray threads trailing on the floor. All nine classrooms were decorated with Chinese calligraphy and arithmetic problems. Maps were drawn on the blackboards. In the senior classroom, a simple lesson in English was put up.

With 700 enthusiastic, expectant cleaners, tidiers and organizers, most of these preparations were accomplished in a few frenzied hours. "Everyone," says Mills, "from the youngest to the eldest, knew his responsibility and what had to be done." It was not even necessary for any of the 50 or so adults on staff to monitor the cleanup. "If any of the children shirked his or her duty, the rest of them sure told him about it," Mills recalls. "In China, no one—not even a five-year-old—wants to lose face."

As it turns out, the initiative, energy, and sense of personal responsibility these children displayed are the very qualities CCF has continued to promote among its beneficiaries. In those early years when "CCF" still stood for China's Children Fund, the children were seen, and were encouraged to see themselves, as precisely that– beneficiaries. Gratitude for benefactions, even reverence for the bene- factor, was the order of the day. Today, the emphasis is on the achievements of the beneficiaries. Nevertheless, visitors to CCF projects– especially if they are foreigners–are invariably received with formal ceremonies of respect, ranging from tea and cakes to huge assemblies of awestruck children (whose awe soon dissolves into giggles). Digni- fied parents and slightly anxious staff members join in for traditional presentations of garlands. Not infrequently, welcoming signs incorpo- rating the visitor's name are evident. Often the welcoming ceremonies take on a life of their own, with children performing carefully rehearsed dances or songs, and become a kind of festival—a joyful suspension of the day's routine.

Finally the great day arrived. When Erwin Raetz drove up in a jeep with Clarke on that muggy summer afternoon, all 700 children were lined up on the playing field like a little army in their new khaki uniforms. In the front row, the smallest children waved triangular paper flags that said in English, "Welcome, Dr. Clarke." A large banner of white cloth had been painted by one of the teachers famous for his calligraphy. Hanging across the top of the main gate, the banner read in Chinese and English, "Welcome to our great benefactor Dr. J. Calvitt Clarke." The teachers and all the other staff were lined up on either side of the front walk leading to the door. No Roman emperor ever received more elaborate homage.

"A speech of welcome written by one of the teachers had been memorized days before by one of the older boys," Mills remembers. "He delivered it with the gusto and eloquence of a professional orator. We were all so proud of him. He was probably 12 or 13, and he was not a bit nervous.

"One of the smaller girls had been chosen to present a bouquet of flowers to Dr. Clarke. A beautiful new dress had been made for the occasion, and a red ribbon tied in her hair. She was only a little one of six or seven. Shyly, she walked toward Dr. Clarke, looking down on the ground most of the time, well aware that the eyes of over 700 people were upon her. She placed her flowers in Dr. Clarke's hands, and in a trembling little voice spoke her memorized piece in English: 'Dr. Clarke, we the children of KuKong Home present these flowers to you with much gratitude, and we love you.' It was obvious that Dr. Clarke was deeply moved. With tears in his eyes, he bent down and put his arms around her and kissed her on the forehead.

"Immediately a subdued chuckle went through the whole group of children. They had never witnessed anything like this before. In China, we do not express our emotions with such visible manifestations of affection. Nevertheless, the children recognized the language of love and knew that here was a man who really cared for them."

Mills and the children learned something from Clarke's visit that radically changed their relationship with CCF. Clarke's first words to the assembled children, Mills remembers, were, "I bring to you all loving greetings from each of your 'adoptive parents' in America."

There was silence. Seven hundred children waited expectantly for Mills, who was acting as interpreter, to translate, but he didn't know what to say. "I was puzzled by this statement," he recalls, "as to how I should word it in Chinese. Up until this time I thought China's Children Fund had adopted us collectively in a purely financial sense. I was not aware that each child had an 'adoptive parent' somewhere in the United States."

At this early stage, there was as yet no contact between "adoptive parents" and their "adopted children." Later, when the concept changed from "adoption" to "sponsorship," relationships based on the exchange of letters would become a critically important component of CCF's work. But at this moment, standing in the playing field with his 700 charges under the hot South China sun and hearing about "adoptive parents" for the first time, Mills was introduced to a whole new idea.

"It's true we had sent pictures of each of the children with a case history," he says. "But I thought this was necessary so that the organization would know that the funds remitted were actually helping to support the stated number of children. After a few words of explanation from Dr. Clarke, I saw the light, came to life and explained what Dr. Clark was saying to the children. What a brilliant idea it was: Each child in the home had a friend in America who was interested in their welfare! How wonderful! I realized how far-reaching this would be in giving each child a feeling of security. They had no family, but now they knew they had someone far away who loved and cared for them."

With this new knowledge and its implications taking root in the minds of the children, Mills accompanied Dr. Clarke on a tour of the orphanage. Despite the outstanding success of The Big Wash, it was not the cleanliness, neatness, and shine that most impressed his guest, but, rather, the vocational training workshops.

"The two vocational classrooms had been readied for inspection," says Dr. Mills. "The boys were working with the lathes, the shaper and the drill presses. Instructors explained how the milling machine cut gears into unfinished metal stock. On the far side of the room, several old truck engines were on the floor in various stages of reassembly. They were being used to teach the older boys automobile mechanics. The boys were very proud of their workshop, and were always anxious to show visitors what they could do.

"In the next room, the 12 big wooden hand looms were lined up in two rows of six, with a girl sitting at each loom, weaving the cotton thread into toweling and plain white cloth. It was most fascinating to watch the girls coordinating the movement of the foot pedals, causing the warp to open half up and half down, so that the shuttle could shoot from one side to the other as the cotton yarn was woven into a beautiful fabric, one thread at a time."

What Dr. Clarke saw in those two vocational training classrooms was much more than "charity." The machines gave the children the means to meet their own needs in the future—to provide for their own families, to become productive, responsible members of their communities—all despite the fact that they were orphan "outcasts."

"This is what is needed in all the orphanages in China," Clarke told Mills at dinner that night. "Would you consider coming to China's Children Fund, working with us, and organizing this in all our homes?"

~~~

The meeting of Clarke and Mills in Canton in 1946 was both the culmination of CCF's beginnings and the opening of its new future. There came together the two individuals who have done more than anyone else to create and sustain CCF as a vibrant force for the welfare of children throughout the world. Although others would come along to make significant contributions, it was Clarke who conceived the unique engine and got it going, who sold the idea to thousands upon thousands of Americans, and who assured a steady stream of both sponsors and sponsorship funds. And it was Mills who would make use of his experiences in war-ravaged China to ensure that CCF did much more than merely collect together homeless and hapless children. It was his vision and commitment that CCF's work was only beginning when each sponsored child was housed, clothed, and fed. There was a vital human being ready to be nurtured in learning, skills, and values. If Clarke had a dream to save the suffering children of the world, Mills had a plan to make them whole beings.

The stage was already being set for CCF not only to expand constantly outward, but also to make a significant contribution to the whole lives of thousands of children.

Chapter Two

AFTERMATH OF WAR, 1947-1951

Shanghai, China—1947

Verent Mills was taken aback by Calvitt Clarke's invitation to join China's Children Fund and to take over the development of training programs at CCF's growing number of orphanages. Such an idea had never entered his mind. But since he and his wife, the former Alma Kenney of Winnipeg, and their three children were due to return to Canada the following year, it was a propitious time for him to consider the possibilities. Mills promised he would visit Richmond at that time and give Clarke an answer.

During 1947 while on his furlough in Canada, Mills bought a bus ticket from Toronto to Richmond, Virginia; he had obtained the blessing of his mission board to pursue Clarke's offer. After an eventful trip across the Mason-Dixon line where he learned about Jim Crow seating arrangements on public buses, Mills had his first encounter with CCF in Richmond.

He met with Clarke and his wife, Helen. Blonde, attractive, and energetic, Helen Clarke was not shy. A native of Irwin, Pennsylvania, and well educated at the University of Pittsburgh, she became active at the very heart of the CCF operation, first as a volunteer and then from January 1942, as a salaried "assistant to the Executive Director." The offices of China's Children Fund were located on the corner of Fifth and Main Streets. Board meetings were still being held in a private dining room of the Occidental Restaurant on North Eighth Street.[1]

---

[1] CCF Executive Committee Minutes, January 9, 1942.

"Dr. Clarke had called a special meeting of the board," Mills recalls. "Mr. [Verbon] Kemp, who was one of the directors at the time and also executive director of the Virginia State Chamber of Commerce, moved that 'the board of China's Children Fund employ Mr. Mills as overseas director, to direct our work in the field.' The vote in favor was unanimous."

The actual title of Overseas Director, however, was retained for the time being by Erwin Raetz, the minister of the Dutch Reformed Church who had first told Mills about CCF. The number of CCF-supported orphanages scattered across the vast expanse of China would increase from 21 to 42 between 1946 and 1949. As these institutions required plenty of supervision, Mills was put in charge of North China, while Rev. Raetz remained in the South. In addition, reports were reaching Richmond of hungry, homeless orphans in war-ravaged Japan and Korea. It was decided that Mills would expand CCF's activities into these countries, and he was invited to become director of North China, Korea, and Japan.

In January of 1948, Mills and his family returned to China—this time to the teeming, bustling, cosmopolitan port city of Shanghai, on the coast of central China. From there, Mills set to work scouting new orphanages for CCF to assist in the northern provinces, where the devastation from the Japanese invasion was greatest.

"The whole country was ravaged," says Mills. "It was desolation. I went out, and I found various people who were taking care of children and who wanted help: missionaries, Chinese church people. They already had orphanages, but they needed money." Of the ten new institutions Mills enrolled for CCF, some were small: 40 or 50 children being cared for in cramped quarters or a private home. Others, like the one in Chengdu in Szechwan province, more than 1,000 miles west of Shanghai, had as many as 140 children living in dormitories. Four small orphanages—one of them a babies' home—were right in Shanghai.

Conditions in the orphanages were spartan, but the buildings— many of centuries-old Chinese brick—were solid. Three of the homes were in new buildings whose construction was funded by CCF. At this point, CCF was receiving about $480,000 a year in contributions. The steady stream of personal letters from Dr. and Mrs. Clarke to a wide spectrum of Americans was achieving an abundant response. Clarke's fundraising prowess was utterly amazing, providing almost unlimited opportunities in assisting distressed children throughout China and Japan.

Mills had a happy challenge on his hands. "I lined up homes as quickly as I could for Dr. Clarke," Mills remembers. "He would send me cables that would burn up if they were written on asbestos: 'Need 4,000 more children! Get more homes for CCF to sponsor! We've got more requests than we have children!' I couldn't even get the case histories and everything typed up from one home before I'd get another cable asking for 2,000 more children! The sponsors were already in, they'd sent their money, and he didn't have the pictures of children to send to them. He said the people were responding so fast because they wanted to have a part in the rehabilitation of China."

But Mills also took very seriously the other part of his responsibilities as overseas director—the development of homes and training programs. He established high standards for the care of his charges; most of these were the outcome of his personal experience. He was determined to ensure that the children in CCF homes were properly cared for in a variety of specific ways. For example, by assessing and analyzing the amount of care the children actually needed, Mills established the policy of a children-to-staff ratio of 11 to one in the orphanages, and five to one in the babies' homes. There had to be a bed for each child, and there had to be adequate sanitary facilities—which in China in those days meant the availability of wooden buckets—indoors. One orphanage in Shanghai actually had flush toilets; in Chengdu and Peking, farmers came around and collected the night soil every morning. In all the orphanages but one, water had to be carried in from rivers or wells, and heated on stoves for bathing in winter. None of the homes had central heating, and padded cotton coats were provided for the children in winter. Mills insisted that each child had to have access to a washbasin, and have his own towel and toothbrush. Eventually, even toothpaste was provided.

Mills also wanted to ensure that all the children of school age went to school. Some of the homes, such as the Canaan Home in Shanghai, had their own schools. In the others, children attended nearby schools and CCF paid the tuition. Mills was not in North China long enough to set up vocational training programs in any of the orphanages there, as he had earlier in Canton, but he says he did learn an important lesson in child development from the experience of Shanghai's Canaan Home.

The Canaan Home was, in Mills' words, "strictly a church-operated orphanage"—a self-contained world with its own school and its own church, as well as living quarters for the children. As a result, according to Mills, the children in the Canaan Home were ill-prepared to face the outside world once they "graduated."

"We had lots of problems with those kids," he remembers. "They had been isolated from the community, and they couldn't adjust to being outside. They stopped going to church, they found it difficult to find jobs, they didn't know the outside customs, they were maladjusted." As a result, Mills concluded that the orphanages should not have "in house" schools and that church services should not regularly take place within the institutions. Bible studies and devotions were appropriate, but on Sunday the children should go out to the church of their own choice.

In later years, as CCF began assisting children within their own families, rather than in institutions, whatever explicitly religious content there had been in the organization's work would disappear, except in cases where a CCF project was affiliated with a local religious group. The underlying Christian motivation for CCF's work, however, has remained intact. In non-Christian communities, CCF policy has long discouraged activities that could be regarded as proselytizing. Indeed, CCF's continued welcome in many communities has been assured by a strict adherence to this policy.

Another long-standing practice of CCF—"adoption"—was also critically important to Mills as he organized the growing number of homes under his charge. While CCF sponsors responded to the Clarkes' pleas to "adopt" their very own child somewhere across the sea, the adopted child also could easily relate to the idea. After the terror and wrenching sadness of losing their families in the war, this sense of connection with an adult far away—someone who cared about them and wrote them letters—was more important to many of these lonely children than all the blankets, rice and clean water the orphanages could provide.

"For the children it was a wonderful thing," Mills recalls, "because they didn't have anyone else. They said to themselves, 'Here's somebody way over in America who really loves me, who thinks of me.' It gave them a feeling of security, of being wanted. This is what we hoped to develop. You'd go into the orphanages, and the children would have a picture of their sponsor up on the wall behind the bed. And the sponsors would send gifts on the children's birthdays too. Nobody had ever remembered the birthdays of these children before."

Unfortunately, the bonds between thousands of Chinese children and their CCF sponsors were soon to be abruptly severed. By December 1949, when the Communists seized power in China, CCF sponsors were assisting 5,113 children in 42 homes throughout the country. Mills had expected that Mao Tse-tung's Red Army would prevail over the Nationalist forces of Chiang Kai-shek: he had even been reading books on Marxism and Leninism, "so that," as he puts it, "to a certain degree, I could meet them on their own ground intellectually." What he had not expected was that the work of CCF would no longer be welcome under the new regime.

Mills agreed with the Communists on one important point: change was needed in China. Ever since the revolution of 1911 brought down the last ruling dynasty, the political pendulum had been wildly swinging from left to right, creating great instability. The country was controlled for all practical purposes by five feudal lords who taxed the peasants unmercifully. "There wasn't oppression as such," says Dr. Mills. "People were free to come and go as they pleased. But the taxation of the warlords brought great hardship to a country where most people were already very poor. The Communists wanted to give the peasants an opportunity for a better life."

At their home in Shanghai in the Spring of 1949, the Millses and their children listened to daily radio reports about the advance of the Communist forces. Before long, the family could hear artillery shells exploding in the distance: The sound grew closer, and more menacing, by the day. The Communists had crossed the Yellow River. Nanking, at that time the Chinese capital, was expected to fall any day. It was clear from the heavy traffic on the river that the central government was evacuating Nanking, but no one yet knew where it planned to go. Some people speculated that Chiang Kai-shek would try to resist the Communists in Canton. It was only after the fall of Shanghai four weeks later that Mills learned that the government had retreated to the island of Formosa (Taiwan).

Foreigners and wealthy Chinese were rushing to leave Shanghai by sea and by air, but Mills and his family—along with a small handful of other foreigners, mostly missionaries—wanted to stay on. "Alma and I were going to remain and take care of the children," he says. "We had these 5,000 kids in China, and I wasn't going to run off and leave them. We loved those kids, and we thought that after yet another war, the children would need our help more than ever."

As the sound of artillery fire grew closer, a stream of terrified peasants began pouring into the city, carrying all their possessions on hand-drawn carts. Nationalist soldiers fleeing the fighting soon followed. They would change into civilian clothes as soon as they could to avoid detection by the advancing Red Army troops. By now, there was no escape from Shanghai. All the ships had sailed, and the fuel at the airport had been burned by Communist agents. The city, swollen by countless newly arriving refugees, could only wait nervously for the Red Army to march in.

It so happened that the Millses' house was next to the park where the Nationalist soldiers fought their last battle against the Communist troops. For days, the family huddled under the dining room table to escape falling plaster. Finally, a deathly quiet settled over the area, more frightening at first than the incessant pounding of artillery had been. The next day, Mills, still believing he would be welcomed by the Communists, piled his wife and three children in the family car and set out to check on friends living in another section of the city. Emerging from their driveway, the Millses were waved forward by a rifle-bearing soldier with a red star on the front of his khaki-green cap.

"Driving down the main thoroughfare," Mills recalls, "there was devastation everywhere. The overhead trolley wires and power lines were down; telephone poles were broken and windows were shattered. Abandoned military equipment and dead horses blocked many of the side streets. Litter was scattered everywhere. We drove on cautiously, making our way through the many obstructions. Near the main post office, a contingent of soldiers was marching past the intersection. I stopped. A young officer ran up, stopped his troops, parted the ranks and signaled us to drive through.

"In time we reached our destination and found our friends safe. As we returned home in the afternoon, we found to our utter amazement that the streets had been cleaned and that some of the streetcars were already running again. Shops were opening for business and soldiers could be seen everywhere with their bamboo brooms, sweeping the streets and clearing away the debris. In just a few days the city was cleaner than it had been for months."

Mills then sent a cable to Dr. Clarke in Richmond. "All safe and well," it read. "Future looks promising."

He then went to withdraw some money from one of the Shanghai branches of the Chase Manhattan bank. He stopped to talk to the American manager of the branch, who was full of admiration for the behavior of the Communist troops. "Mills," he said, "in all my years in China I have never seen anything like this. These soldiers are disciplined and their conduct is exemplary. If this is Communism, they can put anything on their ticket and I'll sign it."

A month after the Communists took over the city, they held a victory parade. According to local custom, shopkeepers lined the streets, offering the soldiers gifts: towels, toothpaste, soap, liquor—whatever there was in stock. But the rapaciousness expected of a conquering army never materialized: The soldiers marching by would have none of it. "We are well provided for," they told the merchants. "Give it to the poor!"

Mills' work with the three Shanghai orphanages continued. Before the arrival of the Red Army, he had brought the rice supply from the Bethel Home and stored it for safekeeping on his own veranda. But after observing the Army's order and discipline, Mills returned the rice to the orphanage.

Six weeks after entering Shanghai, the army moved on to capture

South China from the remaining Nationalist forces. In the Army's wake came the political cadres of the Communist Party, and the situation in Shanghai changed overnight. Suddenly, piles of books could be seen burning in the streets, and walls were plastered with huge banners and billboards shrieking such slogans as: "Down with capitalism!" "Death to the running dogs of imperialism!" "Obliterate colonialism!" "The People will rise above tyranny!"

Then followed what was called, with gruesome irony, The Flowing of Flowers. Lawyers, teachers, former government employees and wealthy landlords were shot in the public squares, and citizens were called out of their homes to witness the spectacle.

"The lawyers were the first to be cleared out," Mills recalls. "Day after day we saw people being shot right in the street: public executions. After the lawyers came the big landowners, and then the intelligentsia. They were all caught up in capitalism and foreign connections, so they were cleaned off."

Mills and his wife were required to come out to watch the executions along with everyone else. Terrible as this was, it was an occurrence they had seen countless times in the past. "When I first went to China in '31, in the town where we lived every fifth store was an opium den," he says. "There were opium smokers everywhere. The central government passed an edict that the dens were to be closed, and that the addicts had to go to the hospital for treatment. This was a very enlightened policy. The only thing was, if a rehabilitated addict was caught smoking opium, he or she was executed. It was a brutal response, but it got rid of the drug problem in a hurry."

Under the newly arrived Communists, foreign businesses, of which there were were many in Shanghai, were closed. The local power structure was rigidly organized, from the mayor down to "neighborhood officers," each of whom was responsible for keeping track of the movements of ten families—including foreigners. No member of the Mills family could leave the house without first informing the neighborhood officer. Everyone in the city received identity cards, and was instructed to carry them at all times and to memorize the numbers in case the cards were lost.

"One day I was told to go to police headquarters," says Mills. "The officials there claimed that I was an international spy and that I was setting up orphanages as a cover for my work as a 'running dog of the imperialists.' That's the expression they used.

"They were calling everybody a spy," says Mills. "Their manner was domineering, but it didn't worry me. Everybody knew what I had been doing. I had nothing to hide. My conscience was clear. I gave my accusers a list of the CCF homes in Shanghai, and the response was:

'You don't need to worry, the Communist government is more than capable of taking care of its children.' Soon, we received word from Canton that the government was confiscating all our properties.

"The Communists put their own personnel in charge of the orphanages," says Mills. "Some of our staff remained in subordinate positions, but the cadres were in charge and we soon found out that the children, even the very young ones, were being subjected to intensive political indoctrination—brainwashing. To the Chinese Communists, an orphan was a prized possession because he didn't have a family to bind him. The authorities could take these young people and educate them and make them good cadres." Under the new regime, the orphanages were called Children's Productive Societies, and the children were put to work making grass mats and sandals for the soldiers.

By this time, the Millses realized there was nothing they could do to help the orphans in the 11 facilities scattered across North China. The authorities would not permit Mills to visit the homes or to have any contact with them. It was clear that in the new China, Westerners would not be welcome, and the Millses decided to apply for exit visas. Indeed, all foreign CCF personnel were eventually forced to leave the country.

Then the ordeal began. It took more than ten days of standing in long lines with Chinese citizens desperate for exit visas before Mills was able to see someone at police headquarters about obtaining visas for himself and his family.

"When I finally got to see someone," Mills recalls, "I was informed that I would be required to write a history of my years in China from the time of my arrival in 1931 until the present, 1949—a period of 18 years! This was supposed to be a week-by-week chronicle: I was expected to list every place I had lived in China, the names and addresses of everyone with whom I worked for nearly two decades; I had to describe what I did, where my money came from, and so on."

Mills worked for weeks on this task, but predictably, there were many things he could not recall. Just as predictably, he was summoned by the authorities and told that his document was incomplete.

Explaining that he simply could not remember everything, Mills received a sinister smile from his examiner. "Don't worry about that; you have plenty of time to think about it. Take it home and in time it will come to you." From this point on, Mills' history was liberally sprinkled with fiction.

During the four months he waited to leave China, Mills was filled with sadness for the thousands of children he would leave behind. But he says he had no fear for his personal safety or that of his family, only a sense of helplessness and frustration.

"We were doing as we were told," he explains. "When the army left, some soldiers remained behind, and they made us feel secure. There was peace and quiet on the streets: it was safer than before."

Nevertheless, on five separate occasions, Communist military personnel made unscheduled visits to the Millses' home. "Each time," Mills recalls, "the entire house was searched—the dressers, cupboards, everything. I was afraid they would plant a gun to incriminate me, but they never did. Everything was left neat and tidy. They were well disciplined. There was no monkey business; it was just one question after another."

The next step in the exit procedure required Mills to place a daily announcement in each of the four Shanghai newspapers for a period of two weeks, stating that he intended to leave China and asking anyone who knew of any reason why he should not be issued an exit visa to come forward. The announcements had to be clipped and pasted in a scrapbook as proof of compliance.

The authorities also asked Mills to produce a notarized letter stating that financial support for all the CCF orphanages would continue to arrive from the United States for the next six months. But because the U.S. government had now barred the remittance of funds to all Communist countries, Dr. Clarke and T. Nelson Parker, the president of CCF, had to travel to Washington to obtain special permission from the State Department to send money to the Bank of China. Mills believes the money was actually remitted to the orphanages. "At that time," he says, "they were very gung ho about doing things right." Still, the exit visa was not forthcoming.

Instead, government officials now demanded that Mills obtain a "shop guarantee"—an affidavit from a Shanghai shopkeeper expressing a willingness to assume responsibility for any and all unpaid debts the Millses might leave behind. Mills was in despair. How would he possibly find a Chinese willing to compromise his own position in those dangerous days by vouching for a "foreign devil"?

He told Mr. Chang, the CCF business manager in Shanghai, of his dilemma. Miraculously, Chang soon produced an impressive document signed and sealed by a man who owned an office supply business, a close friend of his late father. Mr. Chang's father had been a Methodist minister in Shanghai, and his son had no trouble convincing the shop owner, a deacon in the same church, to vouch for Mills. "I know Pastor Mills and I will put my life on the line for him," the shopkeeper declared. "If anything comes up, I will be personally responsible."

The official to whom Mills presented this affidavit looked so astonished and impressed that Mills felt sure he and his family would at last be free to leave China. Indeed, he was told to pack his belongings at once and to return for the visa the following week.

However, when Mills returned, he was informed that his visa could not be issued until certain "labor problems" were resolved. This final hurdle was overcome only when a high-ranking bureaucrat whom Mills had known in Canton discovered that it was another Mills, the editor of *The Shanghai Post and Mercury*, who was having labor problems with his employees.

Finally, four months after the Millses had decided to leave China, the truck that would transport them and other refugees to a waiting ship pulled up outside their home. Each family member was permitted to bring only two suitcases. Most of the possessions accumulated over 18 years of living in China were left behind.

The tension was palpable as the ship slipped down the Wangpo River and into the Yangtse delta that afternoon. One man, who had been about to leave with his wife and small son, was detained by officials at the last moment. His wife, pleading to be allowed to stay behind with her husband, was forced aboard the ship with the child.

"It was only when the captain announced that the ship had reached international waters," says Mills, "that the passengers began at last to believe that they were free.

"What worried me more than anything was whether we would ever have the opportunity to come back," he says. "After we left, I felt that if the Nationalists didn't retake the country in three years, it would take another 30 years. For a while, it looked like things were changing in China, but with Tiananmen Square, the whole place is bolted down again."

It is not known what happened to most of the 5,113 children in China's CCF orphanages—or whether the institutions continued to function as orphanages after 1949, and if so, whether they continued to receive adequate support from the new government. For the new, rabidly anticolonialist regime, any connection with foreign churches smacked of imperialism, and had to be rooted out. One thing is certain: All contact between the children and their American sponsors was cut off.

Mills does know what happened to a number of the children whom he had personally rescued from starvation and brought to the orphanage in Canton in 1945. At least 300 managed to walk more than 60 miles down the Canton-Hong Kong railroad line when the Communists took power and to cross over the border into Hong Kong.

"Of the original 700 that I picked up," says Dr. Mills, "about 280 are still in Hong Kong. Five are ordained pastors, having gone through seminary, and another 25 are involved in Christian education. There are nine doctors, four dentists, and three college professors. We have school principals—I don't remember how many, and many teachers. We have boys who are in the Hong Kong immigration service and the Hong Kong police force. Some of the girls are nurses. There are boys in construction, and others are mechanics and things like that. And there are two who are millionaires."

When, in 1980, Dr. and Mrs. Mills returned to Hong Kong after an absence of several years, the original orphans held a huge banquet in their honor.

"After the speeches," Mills recalls, "one of the boys, who today owns a big restaurant and is very wealthy, walked over to our table and said, 'Pastor, I just wanted to say thank you for what you did for me when I was a little boy. Everything I have today is because of you.'

"That touched me very deeply, and for a moment I couldn't respond. Finally I said to him, 'Yung Wai, it isn't me, it's because God loves us. God loves you, God loves me. Through God's providence we were permitted on this land. So we must thank God, and nobody else. God is the one who has loved us, and has taken care of us.'

"Later in the evening, one of the boys announced that the grandchildren were going to sing for Grandpa and Grandma, meaning us. The little kids were sitting there in front of us, singing all these little choruses that I'd taught their grandparents: 'This Little Light of Mine,' 'Jesus Wants Me for a Sunbeam,' and 'Jesus Loves Me.' The parents had passed it on to the second and third generations."

When Mills describes his 18 years in China, he likes to quote a Chinese proverb. He says it illustrates his sense of CCF's philosophy and of the enduring effect of its work. "If you plant for a year," says Dr. Mills, "you plant grain. If you plant for ten years, you plant a tree. But if you plant for a hundred years, you plant men."

~~~

Seoul, Korea—1948

The late 1940s were also very bad years for Koreans, and especially for Korean children. When Japan lost the War in 1945, Korea was freed from 35 years of brutal Japanese occupation, only to be summarily chopped in half at the 38th parallel and divided into opposing spheres of influence by the world's great powers. Korea's industrialized, resource-rich North was handed over to the control of the Soviet Union; the impoverished, underdeveloped South, to the United States.

Poverty in a cold climate is particularly cruel: Malnourished people, huddled in unheated, makeshift shacks and dressed in little more than rags, can mount little resistance to biting winter winds and snow. In Korea, many died, leaving their children to fend for themselves.

31

Mothers who despaired of feeding yet another baby would abandon their infants in public places, hoping that someone would give their children a home.

Economic stagnation and political instability made life hard for everyone, particularly the hordes of refugees pouring south from the Communist-held North. It is estimated that six million people crossed into South Korea between 1945 and 1949, cramming two thirds of Korea's population into what was then the poorer section of the country. In Seoul, half the inhabitants were refugees, and starving, homeless children were dying of exposure, huddled in doorways all night long, trying to get away from the snow. Little girls became prostitutes in order to survive; little boys became skillful, practiced thieves. Gangs of filthy, emaciated children roamed the streets, sleeping in alleyways and preying on passersby.

The South Korean government, headed by Syngman Rhee, had other problems, other priorities, and in any case, was totally unequipped to deal with tens of thousands of uncared-for, parentless children. Foreign missionaries and concerned Koreans did what they could. The former took waifs into their homes by the score, while the latter set up orphanages in Buddhist temples and abandoned buildings, and even carved shelters into rocky hillsides. But the need far outstripped the means at hand. As word of the suffering got out, the crisis presented a compelling opportunity to Dr. Clarke and his willing sponsors. In the fall of 1948, Verent Mills was sent from his base in Shanghai, China, to Korea to take stock of the situation. On that first trip he signed up five orphanages for assistance by China's Children Fund.

All but one of these homes were run by Christian missionaries such as the Underwoods, whose family had been in Korea since the 1880s. Ethel Underwood (her husband was a member of the Underwood Typewriter family) was particularly concerned at this time about the plight of the country's abused and exploited orphan girls. These "superfluous" daughters of the poor—often no more than ten years old—were sent by their families to work as housemaids. Frequently, ties with their families were broken, and the girls would be entirely at the mercy of their new "masters." Many were eventually turned out into the street. To care for these girls, Mrs. Underwood had, a few years earlier, founded the Ethel Underwood Home, which CCF was eager to assist. Her husband, Horace Underwood, was made Chairman of the Board of the Korean branch of China's Children Fund.

Another CCF-assisted home was established by Mrs. Harry J. Hill, a Presbyterian leader in the town of Chongju some 75 miles southeast of Seoul. It provided shelter, food, education and even vocational training for a group of orphans who were traditionally considered worthless and expendable in the Far East: the blind. There, blind children operated knitting machines, farmed, performed calisthenics, played baseball, and outscored sighted children on national academic exams. Eventually CCF would establish two more homes for blind orphans in Korea.

One of the first Korean orphanages assisted by CCF, the Christian Children's Home, was founded by a venerable Korean physician, Dr. K.S. Oh, in An Yang, just south of Seoul. Already in his mid-seventies, Dr. Oh was a graduate of the University of Louisville in the Kentucky city of that name. He would continue as director of the home until he was well into his eighties. Later, this institution would serve as a laboratory for a revolutionary experiment in institutional child care.

But those days were yet to come. Conditions in Korean orphanages in the late 1940s were primitive and the staff severely overtaxed, but willing. What staff there was consisted of devoted, but untrained individuals. Child psychology, early childhood development and child welfare were only just emerging as distinct fields of study in the West—and were almost unheard of in Korea.

In the meantime Korea, hobbled by decades of foreign exploitation and economic distress, was beginning to feel the rumblings of an even greater devastation. The Communists in the North, backed by the Soviet Union, began infiltrating the South. Incidents of violence became more and more common.

On March 17, 1949, Communist guerrillas broke into the Underwood home in Seoul and shot and killed Ethel Underwood. It was said later that the assassins had deliberately targeted the most beloved American in Korea to show their contempt for the United States. By December 1949, CCF was assisting orphanages throughout Korea. The following June, the North Korean army marched into Seoul, prompting United Nations troops and American peacekeeping forces to be rushed to the aid of the South Koreans. The country was at war with itself.

For the next three years, the Korean War swept back and forth, up and down across the midsection of the country like a square dance of death. In the three months between June and September 1950, Seoul was captured by the North, retaken by the South, and lost to the North again. On the South Korean side alone, nearly two million Koreans died in the conflict. As always, those who suffered most from battles and bombings, confusion and deprivation were children. Even the children in CCF-assisted orphanages were vulnerable. Homes in occupied territory were evacuated before the Communist advance. Their fleeing children once again joined the ragged ranks of frightened, hungry refugees. For a lucky few trekking through the devastated countryside, sustenance came in the unlikely form of K rations supplied by American GIs.

By December, the UN troops were being beaten back by Chinese forces who had joined their Communist allies. Painfully, in fear and utter chaos, Seoul was being evacuated yet again. Refugees loaded their possessions onto oxcarts and their babies onto their backs and set out in the bitter cold for unknown havens further south. The UN forces, trying to hold a territorial line of battle, felt compelled to let the throngs of refugees through, and Communist guerrillas—some dressed as women carrying grenades as well as bundled babies—slipped through in the crowds. Soon the Western allies had no alternative but to close the line to Communists and refugees alike. Many of those who remained north of the line were shot.

During the confusion and terror of those days, word of CCF's stranded and endangered orphans reached American fighter pilot Colonel Dean Hess of the Fifth Air Force, originally from Marietta, Ohio, who flew more than 300 combat missions in World War II and the Korean War. He was also a Protestant clergyman who had joined the U.S. Army Air Corps in 1941 because he felt that he could not exhort his parishioners to risk their lives for their country unless he was prepared to do the same. On hearing of the plight of the CCF orphans, Colonel Hess decided he would do whatever was necessary to save them.

Over several tense days in December, close to a thousand children were rounded up in a fleet of trucks and taken to the Seoul air base. They came from Mrs. Hill's Chongju Home for Blind Children and her Chongju Home for Boys, and from a U.S. Army camp where an assortment of homeless waifs had gathered. From there, they were flown in an airlift by U.S. and Korean fighter pilots under Hess's command to Cheju Island, about 60 miles off the south coast of Korea. The rescue came to be known as Operation Kiddie-Car and provided the story for a warm and gripping movie titled *Battle Hymn.*

On Cheju Island, Mills was waiting for the unheated DC-3s and their cargoes of freezing, cold, frightened babies, children and teenagers to arrive. "When we lifted those babies off the planes, whew it was cold!" he says, recalling the tragicomedy of the moment. "The little kids had wet their pants. We were in a sea of cold, wet pants and crying babies."

The only available accommodation for the children on Cheju was an abandoned Japanese agricultural college without a single intact window. Mills and a group of GIs boarded up the windows against the icy wind. But for many of the youngest children, infants already weak from lack of milk, this was not enough. The cold and hunger were too much for them. Two hundred tiny, unmarked graves were dug in the frozen ground of Cheju. Word was sent to Dr. Clarke of the evacuation,

Dr. Verent Mills visiting a CCF Assisted orphanage in Taegu, Korea, 1950

and in a short time, sponsorship aid began pouring in for the survivors.

In mainland Korea, the war raged on. In January of '51 the Red Army was still moving southward, but in March, the UN troops pushed it back, retook Seoul and marched north across the 38th parallel. Thousands of tons of bombs were dropped on Korea during this period, and the resulting devastation was unimaginable: an estimated ten million people in South Korea alone were made homeless. Abandoned babies were found in public places everywhere. Makeshift orphanages were springing up in greater numbers than ever before. By 1951, CCF was assisting 17 orphanages in the ravaged nation.

Sometimes the U.S. Army got into the act. When bombs hit Po Wha Bo Yook Won, an orphanage in Seoul, soldiers from the 17th Infantry loaded the surviving children onto trucks and drove them to safety in a nearby country village. But in war, the actions of even a friendly fighting force can be deadly. In 1952, American pilots inadvertently bombed Dr. Oh's Christian Children's Home in An Yang, killing 86 children. The remainder were evacuated to Cheju Island to wait out the war.

By the summer of 1953 when the Korean war ended, CCF was assisting some 4,000 children in 23 homes, and the need continued to grow. Between 50,000 and 100,000 homeless children were living on the streets and in the alleyways of Seoul alone. More and more Koreans were setting up orphanages, like one young Christian pastor, Mr. Kim, who started a Home in Taejon, a city of packing-case hovels known as the "Hiroshima of Korea." The place had been virtually flattened by bombs. The UN forces' Turkish Brigade helped found an orphanage known as Ankara Children's Garden, in the town of Suwon. CCF added homes for the blind, as well as homes for the children of lepers, and even a home for musically gifted children.

CCF's experiences in Korea following the Second World War were harrowing indeed. Threats and circumstances changed daily. The numbers of homeless children could alter dramatically virtually from day to day. The challenges equaled and in many ways exceeded those faced in China. Yet, in retrospect, Korea was perhaps the place where CCF began to fashion an ability to deal with sudden disaster, to intervene in a timely way to save thousands at risk of exposure and death, and to make use of every available resource to rescue the children. These experiences with crisis would help to inform policies and practices that would enable CCF to intervene in dozens of countries and relieve hundreds of human disasters over the next half century.

~~~

Tokyo, Japan—1948

It is hard to imagine that just a few decades ago Japan, today's economic superpower, lay in ruins, her people hungry, homeless and humiliated, her industrial might destroyed. Among a people known for their decorous manners, diligence, and discipline, children by the thousands were growing up wild in the streets, surviving by their wits. Many of the fathers had not returned from the war; many of the mothers had died of starvation. Girls as young as ten were sold to brothels. Boys were conscripted by criminals and taught to pick pockets. "The need was as great as anywhere in the world," says Verent Mills. "Under the bridges, in the tunnels, everywhere, there were people living in hovels—hungry and cold."

CCF moved quickly to establish homes in Japan for children displaced by the war. The first CCF home was Jiai-no Mura (Merciful Love Village). Supervised by a local group of Americans and Japanese, the home was located on a beautiful tract of land just outside Kumamoto. Here on a gentle slope, with a view of the surrounding mountains, children were provided with a climate of peace and schooling.

Three additional homes for children were soon added. In addition to Jiai-no Mura, there were Bott Memorial Home, Ikusei En and the Mayer Home. Seiji Giga, a veteran of Japan's wrenching war and disasters, was appointed Japanese executive secretary to care for the growing number of CCF homes. Born in 1917, Giga lived through many hardships. His home was destroyed during the earthquake of 1923. During the Great Depression of the 1930s he was forced to leave school and go to work. During the Second World War he frequently raised questions about government policy. After the war, he turned his attention to the homeless—especially the children. That is how he was found by Verent Mills and why he was appointed CCF's liaison in Japan. In a few short years, Giga organized more than 60 orphanages for CCF in Japan.

At first, as in Korea, conditions in the Japanese homes were less than ideal, being spartan, primitive, and cramped. "There was a home—it was just a small house, actually," Mills recalls, "with a mother and another woman helping her, and they had 50 children. The kids slept head-to-toe like sardines on the floor."

CCF assisted many such homemade orphanages especially designed for children of Japanese-American parents, including one established by Madame Miki Sawada, an aristocratic Japanese Christian. Her institution, the Elizabeth Saunders Home, was established specifically to care for "R & R children." These were the abandoned, illegitimate offspring of Japanese women and soldiers of the American occupation forces. Driven by sheer hunger, many families sold their daughters into prostitution. According to one account, a GI could engage a girl and a hotel room for a week for as little as $35. Children resulting from such liaisons were doubly stigmatized in the rigidly conformist society of Japan. In a country that prided itself on its ethnic purity, the fact that these children were both illegitimate and of mixed race brought permanent disgrace on their mothers, who were often forced to abandon them. As *de facto* orphans, with no family to define their status, let alone provide for their needs, such children became virtual nonpersons.

CCF eventually assisted children in more than 60 Japanese orphanages. There was, however, a problem staffing them. There simply were no professional social workers in Japan. To remedy the situation, Japan's national welfare administration in 1949 asked CCF to establish a training college for social welfare workers, caseworkers, and institutional workers in the child care sector—an unusual mark of recognition for a private, foreign agency. The result was Izumi Junior College, Japan's first professional training institution for social workers. Izumi was built next door to CCF's cottage-plan orphanage, the Bott Memorial Home, where students did their internship training. The college to the present provides classes in child welfare, educational psychology, nursing, pediatrics, social work techniques, dietetics, music, and many other practical subjects.

~~~

It was in the aftermath of the Second World War that China's Children Fund found its true calling. In China and Korea the growing international agency learned to deal with crises and with hordes of homeless children. Displaced by Communist governments in China and Korea, CCF clung tenaciously to the children it took in, often moving them out of harm's way hundreds and thousands of miles to safe havens. In those quiet homes, CCF then provided much more than shelter, food, and protection. It attempted to nurture and educate its charges to play a role in their own society.

In Japan, CCF arrived amidst the burning ruins of war and attempted to play a role in rebuilding a proud society. Using a strategy that worked elsewhere, CCF created dozens of homes to care for displaced children—especially children of mixed parentage—until the Japanese government was able to care for its own. While CCF intervened during crises in all three of these nations and while it was forced out of Communist China for the safer confines of Hong Kong and Taiwan, the organization watched the revival of each of these nations until such time as CCF's brand of crisis intervention was no longer needed. Eventually each of these nations was able to recover economically, take over CCF's welfare operations, and contribute positively to the condition of children elsewhere in the world. That is one of the most inspiring stories of CCF's first half-century of existence.

Another significant change came out of CCF's work in Korea and Japan. By the early 1950s, China's Children Fund was operating in Japan, Korea, Hong Kong, Taiwan, and India, but no longer in China. It was particularly the Japanese, however, who noted that the name China's Children Fund was no longer appropriate. Verent Mills passed the recommendation on to Calvitt Clarke with a telling comment: "You know, these folk are really chafing with our name. In India they're saying, 'We're not Chinese.' The Koreans are saying, 'We're not Chinese.' The Japanese, they want to forget China. We should change the name."

Although many at CCF feared the loss of recognition involved with a name change, the time had come by 1951 to take the leap. Fortunately a good solution was found. The initials—CCF—would be retained, but from then on, the letters would stand for Christian Children's Fund. On February 6, 1951, CCF's board of directors made the new name official.

The only complaint about the change in CCF's files was reported by Verent Mills from his post in Hong Kong. The government of Indonesia registered its concern. "I had to go to the Ministry of Religion," Mills recalled years later, "and explain that although we operated on the Christian principle of loving thy neighbor, we did not and would not proselytize. Our policy was—and still is—to help children, no matter what faith they belong to. The Ministry accepted this, and CCF is registered in Indonesia."

Chapter Three

FROM ORPHANAGE TO EDUCATION, 1951-1959

Hong Kong—1951

"I felt abandoned," says Chun Wai Chan. "I couldn't understand why I had to be the one to go."

Dr. Chan is Chief of Cardiology at the Kaiser Permanente medical facility in Fresno, California. He is a graduate of Princeton University and Harvard Medical School. He is also a member of the board of directors of Christian Children's Fund. Yet, he can still recall the loneliness and sense of loss he experienced when, as an eight-year-old child in Hong Kong, he was placed in an orphanage by his mother, no longer able to support her six children.

Today, Chan lives with his wife and three children in a spacious, sun-filled, ranch-style house on a quiet, manicured street in suburban Fresno, California, very near the home of former CCF executive director Verent Mills, who is his close friend as well as his patient. But Chan vividly remembers a time when his present life—as a highly trained, respected and prosperous professional with a loving family—was beyond anything he could imagine.

As a child, Chun Wai believed he had been placed in the orphanage because his mother no longer loved or wanted him. This conviction was reinforced when days, weeks, and months went by and she never came to visit him. He didn't learn until later that his mother was unable to visit him because she worked very long hours, sewing sneakers for factories on a piecework basis. And it wasn't until later still that Chun Wai discovered his mother had been compelled legally to give him up in order to place him in the home. The boy, young as he was, had faced change and sorrow before. His father had died two years earlier. When he was six, Chun Wai and his older brother had become the family's principal breadwinners, doing piecework at home. In a city teeming with the cheap labor of millions of refugees from mainland China, this type of work paid next to nothing.

Chun Wai's parents had fled to Hong Kong from Canton when the Communists took power in 1949. He was born two years later. His mother had been a teacher in China, but the government of Hong Kong did not recognize Chinese teaching credentials. With six young children, it was "too hard for her" to go back to school in order to become qualified. Chun Wai's father held a series of jobs. First he imported wine from China; then he opened a small grocery store; finally he sold sponges. "When my father died," says Chun Wai, "we had nothing. My mother had a lot of difficulty finding work, so my brother and I had to go out to the factories."

Listening to Chan today, it is hard to believe that he is talking about himself. The small, soft-spoken, round-faced man radiates a calm self-assurance, and his relaxed, friendly, California style adds to a sense of unreality as he discusses the harshness of his early years.

"We'd often have to visit several different factories to get piecework," he recalls. "Sometimes they'd have work and sometimes they didn't. When they didn't, it meant the family would have nothing to eat."

Chan remembers too that the family lived in "a pretty run-down wooden house." It had a roof made from cardboard boxes that had to be replaced whenever it rained. The one source of hope and comfort, and of occasional handouts of food, was the Christian church the family attended, even though they were not strictly Christians. "I think my family went to church because there was some help available there," he says. "Sometimes, the missionary would come by and see that we were hungry, and he would give us a few dollars out of his own pocket. My mother was a very strong person, and she wanted to hold onto her family. We struggled for two years to try to make it on our own, but we just couldn't do it. Finally my mother asked the missionary to help place the children. In this way, I was sent to an orphanage that was run by Christian Children's Fund."

CCF had started assisting orphanages in Hong Kong in 1951, the year Chun Wai Chan was born, two years after the flood of refugees had begun to pour in from mainland China. Verent Mills and his family had moved to Hong Kong, and there he set up an office as CCF's overseas director, traveling constantly to Korea, Japan, Taiwan, and even Europe and the Middle East.

Between 1949 and 1951, an estimated 2.5 million refugees, like the Chan family, poured into Hong Kong. Many were women whose husbands had been killed by the Communists. To Mills, watching the new arrivals crowding onto the mountainous island and huddling together in flimsy shacks that washed down the hillsides in the typhoons, the most urgent need was to provide a safe and healthy place for the children to live.

"Right after the War, Hong Kong had a population of just one million," according to Mills. "By the mid-fifties, we had at least two and a half to three million more who had come from the mainland. The British were sending them back at the border, but they would come in at night, swimming across the river. The need was appalling—we couldn't build enough homes for them all."

So in 1952, when Chun Wai Chan was a year old, Mills undertook the most ambitious building project CCF has ever funded, before or since: a huge "cottage plan" orphanage called Children's Garden. To this day, it remains Mills' pride and joy.

"When it came to the cottage plan, I had read all I could," says Mills. "I was getting child welfare magazines from England, the United States, and Switzerland." This orphanage would be larger, better designed and better equipped than any in Asia. There would be 12 children to a cottage. Mills was thrilled with the homelike, non-institutional approach of the cottage plan, where each cottage housed a "family"—a "mother" (either a widow or a woman abandoned by her husband) and her 12 "children" of widely ranging ages. Thus would a supportive, loving atmosphere be re-created for desperate children. Mills envisioned a home that would provide far more than just shelter and sustenance. At Children's Garden, the emotional well-being and psychological development of the children would also be of primary importance. However, to become a reality, the project required a substantial amount of real estate.

Mills learned that the government had earmarked a piece of land on a peninsula at the base of Saddleback Mountain to serve as an emergency airstrip. He resolved that this should also be the site of Children's Garden. He, therefore, approached the Governor of Hong Kong, Sir Alexander Grantham, to see what could be arranged.

Sir Alexander, who was not initially very enthusiastic about the project, contacted his superiors at the Colonial Office in London and was told that the land *could* be used as the site of a CCF orphanage— but only if it were acquired via a public auction. At first, Mills felt an insurmountable obstacle had been put in his path. He knew that land was at a tremendous premium in Hong Kong and that CCF would never be able to outbid land developers once news of the auction was released. Such land could easily fetch several hundred dollars a square foot—far more than CCF could afford.

But Mills proved to be a determined and resourceful man. Nothing would stand in his way, or come between his hundreds of refugee orphans and their beautiful new home. The answer, he decided, was to steer real estate speculators away from the land. "I had an architect prepare an elaborate drawing of what Children's Garden would look like spread out on that big bald hillside: the cottages, the kindergarten, the primary school, the vocational high school, the auditorium, the staff quarters, the hospital. Then I invited all the reporters from the English and Chinese dailies in Hong Kong to a banquet in a fine restaurant, and I showed them the drawings and plans.

"Boy, were they impressed. I said to them, 'We're going to buy this land from the government and build this model institution, the largest "cottage plan" child care institution in the Far East. It will be a model of which Hong Kong can be justly proud.' And then I said, 'During the next two weeks, I will be having articles written about this property, what Children's Garden is going to be and what we're going to do for the children. And if you think the project is worth your consideration, we would appreciate it if you would get your papers to print these articles, because we want Hong Kong to know what we're going to do for Hong Kong's orphans.' And for two weeks, the Hong Kong papers were full of our articles.

"Then the day came for the auction. The land office was to open at 2:00 in the afternoon. We were there shortly after 12:00, hoping to be the first so that we could talk to anyone who came along before the auction started. I was going to tell them, 'Look, boys, if you go for this piece of property, you're going to be breaking the rice bowls of your own orphan children here in Hong Kong, whom you could be taking care of instead.'

"Well, 2:00 came, and my colleague and I were the only people there. The district governor hammered down, and the auction started. He read out the description of the land: it runs from here to there, so many hundreds of thousands of square feet from this point to that. Then he said, 'The upset price is ten cents a foot.' "I said, 'I'll take it, sir.'

"'Any further bids?'

"Silence.

"Bang went the gavel! We bought the property for ten cents a square foot, or about $120,000 for nearly 28 acres."

Children's Garden took five years to build. At the grand opening, Mills had a special band flown in all the way from Korea. It consisted of children from CCF's Orphans' Home of Korea — the same children who had been evacuated from Seoul by Colonel Hess in "Operation Kiddie-Car."

At one point over the next few years, Dr. Mills was building three orphanages at the same time—two of them on the cottage plan. Children's Garden, housing more than 1,000 children in 98 cottages, was the largest and the best equipped. Its hospital served not only the children in the orphanage, but area residents as well. In addition to the cottages, elementary school and high school, Children's Garden had superb vocational training facilities. "We had a wood mill," says Dr. Mills, "and a machine shop, and I took great joy in teaching the kids how to run the drill presses and milling machines. We had shoemaking, rattanware, and looms. We made our own cloth, in our own small textile mill."

Mills even used the five-year construction period as a learning experience for the children. "All the land had to be leveled off," says Mills, recalling the period with fondness and pride. "We had our own bulldozers, and I taught our older boys to run them. We did all our own leveling, we made our own topographical map. I had one old mechanic, Leung Gung, and he taught the kids everything. This was teaching them an important trade, the operation and repair of heavy equipment."

Once Children's Garden was fully operative, it was used as a model for other CCF projects. CCF representatives were brought in from Korea, Japan, the Philippines and India for seminars, to see how Children's Garden worked. Among the visitors was Indira Gandhi, who was then the head of the International Union for Child Welfare in India. "So the cottage plan really caught fire," says Mills. "Everybody was for it. The once skeptical Sir Alexander Grantham became the patron of Children's Garden. He took great pride in it."

For Mills, Children's Garden, with its playing fields, its machine shops and its cozy cottages, was the culmination of CCF's work in Asia. Yet it was a most expensive form of assistance to children. The idea of providing Asian orphans with comfortable, homelike accommodations as well as the finest education and vocational training was extravagant. Nevertheless, Mills was convinced these children, if given the very best, would render an ample return on CCF's investment by becoming industrious, responsible citizens of their communities in later years.

Although Children's Garden was a model of its kind, most of the other CCF orphanages in Hong Kong—and in the 15 countries where CCF was working by the mid-fifties—were more like Faith Love, the Hong Kong home where eight-year-old Chun Wai Chan went in 1959. Faith Love, constructed of red brick and reinforced concrete, was clearly a traditional, "no frills" institution.

Dr. Chan remembers how lonely he felt in the unfamiliar surroundings of his new home. The strict regimentation of the orphanage was in sharp contrast to the noisy confusion and intimacy of his mother's tiny house. The little boys slept on barracks-style bunk beds, and their days were precisely structured in near-military fashion.

Chun Wai lived in the Faith Love orphanage for ten years. The rigid discipline that prevailed may have been character-building. But it must have been very hard for six- to eight-year-olds to bear the separation from their families. Although his family was nearby, Chun Wai was permitted to visit them only once a year.

"We'd get up, boys and girls alike, before sunrise and do our morning exercises," Dr. Chan recalls. "All 160 of us would line up with the little water buckets we had been given. After breakfast, we had to clean up the whole orphanage from top to bottom: wash the windows, sweep the floor, mop the floor. I think they thought that if we spent our time cleaning, it would keep us out of trouble.

"Then we'd have morning service. It was not always Christian, although we always sang a hymn and read out loud from the Bible. Sometimes, a teacher would tell us a story about George Washington or Thomas Jefferson or famous Chinese characters. Then from nine to 12 we'd have morning classes. At lunchtime people were assigned to cooking. I learned to cook for 160 people very early in my days."

According to Chan, the food was terrible, but there was more of it and it was more nutritious than the food his mother had been able to provide. "When we had visitors from the United States the food was always better," he recalls. In addition to cooking, Chun Wai learned to grow vegetables, feed pigs, repair furniture, and build water towers— activities all designed to instill self-sufficiency. He was also academically an excellent student.

There were classes morning and afternoon. But at 4:00 p.m. the children were free to play until supper. After supper, they studied in their classrooms until 9:00, when evening prayers began. Once they were back in the dormitory, no talking was allowed. It was a very regimented and totally insulated environment, says Dr. Chan. "We were stigmatized as a result, and treated like aliens. People regarded us as runaways, and there was also antagonism about foreign aid. If you received aid from a foreign country, it meant you were weak, you were not able to support yourself, and your reliance on a foreign person was considered very demeaning for your own culture.

"We had gates right in front of the school, with a sign saying 'ORPHANS' HOME.' There was barbed wire—it was more or less like a correctional institution. Then too, some of us didn't behave; we went out and caused trouble, and that didn't help."

For the first few years, Chun Wai saw his mother, brothers and sisters only once a year, at the time of the Chinese New Year. He dreamed about the visit all year long, yet ironically, when it came, it brought Chun Wai a new source of sadness. "Each time I returned home, I felt less and less like I belonged there," he recalls. "Little by little, I noticed how different I was becoming from the rest of my family. Because of the education and discipline I got, I could handle things better, and I could be very independent."

He would need to call upon this sense of independence very soon, for when he was 12, Chun Wai's mother remarried. His stepfather didn't like the boy, and he was told he would no longer be making his yearly visits home. From then on, Chun Wai's only source of security and self-esteem had to come from the Faith Love Home, which in effect became his family.

"The teachers became very close to us, even though they were very tough on us," says Chan. "Sometimes I would cry and the teachers would try to comfort me. I learned who liked me and who didn't, and who to go to with my problems for emotional support or for guidance: I learned to make the most of whatever was available in the orphanage."

Homes like Faith Love kept children housed, clothed and fed who might otherwise have grown up hungry in the streets. The orphanages offered an education—with the opportunities that implies—to those who were intellectually and psychologically equipped to take advantage of it. Many of the children at Faith Love never did adjust to being there and were never able to benefit from what the institution offered. Instead, these children remained sullen and unhappy, chafing in a perpetual state of resentment and rebellion. Chun Wai came close to joining this group.

"My fourth grade was a terrible year because I was so rebellious," says Chan. "I couldn't understand why I was there. I broke all kinds of rules, did all the terrible things that a boy would do. I would go out to the market and steal things; I would take advantage of the younger kids, punish them, make them my slaves, make them give me things and call them names. I didn't get caught very often.

"Then one day there was an evangelical meeting out in the market that the school superintendant wanted us to go to. We thought, 'Wow, it's a chance to get out of the orphanage! We'll go and steal some more.' So we went to the meeting—it was specially for children. I was very moved by the pastor, and I suddenly realized how badly I was doing. Back at the home, I started to pray and I asked the Lord to forgive me. That was a turning point for me. After that, my behavior and attitude greatly changed. The teachers were very surprised."

Chun Wai was fortunate too that his sponsor, Doris Hawkins, a nurse from Pentwater, Michigan, helped him find the self-confidence he needed, even in the midst of unhappiness. "She was very concerned about how I did in school," he says. "I always got good grades, and she gave me a lot of encouragement when I did well. Sponsorship is very special, because the person is far away and you don't even know what they look like. I would wonder, how come someone who doesn't even know me is willing to help me? Later, I began to think it was just like the love of Jesus Christ. He loves you, not because you're worthy, but just because he loves you. I got to thinking about her a lot, and to really appreciate her when I was about 14 or 15. Later on, I got to know her better as I learned English and could communicate with her directly." Years later in the United States, Chan spent a number of months trying to locate Miss Hawkins. His efforts were finally successful, and they have been in regular contact ever since.

About a third of the children at Faith Love Home never heard from their sponsors, says Chan. But many of these children were the same ones who never took advantage of what the orphanage had to offer. He believes that the children who were most successful later on were those who had close relationships with their sponsors. "Those who never got letters were really miserable," he recalls. "Every month, someone from the CCF Field Office would come to the home to distribute letters and gifts. Everybody would sit down, and there would be a roll call, and when your name was called you felt so happy. I always got something on my birthday and at Christmas, and a card for Valentine's and Easter."

Christmas, in fact, was the high point of the year at Faith Love. It was also one of the few times that Chun Wai had any contact with his future friend, neighbor and heart patient, Verent Mills. "Dr. Mills was very nice to us," he remembers. "Every year, he would come to the Home at Christmas, and we'd have a Christmas banquet, a big roast pig, and Dr. Mills would carve it and hand around the pieces."

Mills remembers Chun Wai from that period too. "I was aware of his standing in school. The home asked me to come at the end of the school year and give out those certificates of academic merit that mean so much to the children. Invariably Chun Wai would run off with two or three of them."

Those were hectic years for Mills. In addition to supervising all of CCF's overseas operations and building orphanages in Hong Kong, he was in charge of yet another CCF experiment to adapt existing child welfare facilities to the need of the hour. This one was designed to respond to the needs of thousands of children living with their families in the horribly cramped conditions of Hong Kong's "H-block" apartment buildings.

"They called them H-blocks because the government had built

them in the shape of an H," says Mills. "Along the long sections there were at least ten 'apartments' consisting of a single nine-by-ten-foot room in which entire families—sometimes as many as ten or 12 people—lived. In the center of the H was a big common kitchen, where the women cooked on their own small kerosene or charcoal stoves, and bathrooms with cold running water. The buildings, which still exist today, were seven and eight stories high. They had electric lights but no elevators. They were made of concrete, and they were pretty dreary."

Bad as they were, says Mills, the H-block buildings were a tremendous improvement over the homemade hillside shacks in which tens of thousands of Hong Kong residents—most of them refugees—had lived previously. "The need for improved housing became desperate after two terrible fires in '55 and '57," says Mills. "The whole mountainside was ablaze in Kowloon. There were few deaths, but in one night, on that one hillside, 65,000 people were made homeless.

"The government built hundreds of H-block buildings," says Mills, "and this helped relieve a critical housing shortage. But at that time, there was no government schooling available for many of the thousands of H-block children. The British only provided schooling for British subjects—children born in Hong Kong—and not many H-block families could afford to send their children to the little private schools that sprang up. So we decided to try and provide schools for the rest on the rooftops of the H-block buildings. We went to the churches and said, 'If you'll find the teachers, CCF will pay their salaries and build the rooftop schools.'"

Ultimately, between seven and eight thousand children were enrolled in the rooftop schools. "Hurricane fence was installed around the edges of the roofs so the kids wouldn't fall off. Four classrooms were built at each end of the roof, and the space between served as a playground." Mills concedes that the curriculum was not as rigorous as in the government schools—the children were not taught English, for example. "But at least they were learning to write their characters and do some arithmetic. The point is that they weren't growing up illiterate and ignorant. If they could read and write, they could get a job in a textile mill, or work in the dockyard, or at the sugar factory, or in home industries. A man could make enough to keep his family in such jobs, but you had to be literate."

Faith Love Home probably provided better schooling than the "rooftop schools," but only through the elementary grades. When the children reached high school age, most of them were transferred to the high school at Children's Garden—but not Chun Wai Chan. It was already clear that Chun Wai was an exceptionally gifted child. The superintendent decided to send him to a first class Christian high school outside the city. Chun Wai's tuition was paid out of sponsorship funds, and he continued to live at Faith Love while commuting back and forth to school by train.

Chun Wai Chan had dreamed of becoming a doctor since the sixth grade, but he felt that because he was an orphan, it would never be possible. Instead, he decided to become a teacher. At the end of tenth grade, he had to prepare for the very challenging Hong Kong citywide college examination. There was only one university in Hong Kong at the time; enrollment was limited, and admission depended on the exam. But Chun Wai did very well and received a scholarship to the university to study chemistry.

According to Chan, the competition was so stiff that only 10 to 15 percent of the children at Faith Love went on to the university. Yet clearly, the Faith Love children received a good education. Among Chan's former classmates are doctors, lawyers, dentists, engineers, economists, computer programmers, and television producers. Even the "rebellious" group who never did well in school were taught practical trades and skills—carpentry, housepainting, farming, auto mechanics—giving them self-sufficiency.

But the CCF orphanages in Hong Kong did more for their children than simply educate them. Regarded, as they were, as social outcasts, Chinese orphans had a special handicap. Chinese employers always wanted to know who a job candidate's family was—who, in effect, would "guarantee" him. Orphans, of course, were not able to produce such guarantors. Dr. Mills, however, devised an effective compensating strategy for his young charges.

"I took a lesson from Dale Carnegie's book *How to Win Friends and Influence People*," Mills recalls. "I'd say to the kids, 'You've got no family, so you have to learn to sell yourselves. When you go to see the *moban*—that's the manager—be frank. Tell him the truth.' Say, 'I've never worked before, but I would like to work for you, and I can promise you that if you'll hire me, I will work as hard as anyone that you have in your factory. And if I don't do a good job, you just tell me and I'll leave.'"

To Americans such advice may sound a bit quaint. But to a young Chinese in Hong Kong in the 1950s, it was truly revolutionary and, as it turned out, highly effective. Nearly all of the orphans in Hong Kong, Korea, Japan and elsewhere who were served by CCF during that period found good jobs upon graduating from the homes.

Mills believed in stressing the "end product" of CCF's work—producing young people who were self-reliant, self-sufficient, responsible citizens. Although CCF no longer assists orphanages, the "end product" concept—the idea that what really matters is how well beneficiaries function once they have moved beyond CCF's orbit—remains paramount in the agency's philosophy.

In the spring of 1968, 17-year-old Chun Wai Chan was headed for Hong Kong University and a teaching career. Then, on the eve of his departure from Faith Love Home, a totally unexpected event occurred. Suddenly, Chun Wai found himself reunited with his mother and siblings he hardly knew. Together they flew to the United States.

The stepfather had recently died. At about the same time, Chun Wai's mother and her father, a resident of the United States since the early 1920s, reestablished contact after a lapse of nearly 40 years. Chun Wai's grandfather arranged for his Hong Kong relatives to emigrate to the U.S.; Chun Wai's great uncle, a waiter in a Chinese restaurant in Queens, arranged a busboy job for him. The day after Chun Wai, his mother, and his two younger sisters arrived in New York, he went to work in the restaurant. He spoke only broken English, and understood almost nothing said to him.

"Initially I was very excited about coming to the United States," Chan remembers. "But when the sun came up the next day, I looked outside—we were in the middle of Harlem where my grandfather lived, because it was much cheaper than Chinatown. I said, 'Oh boy, this is not the United States. This is poverty, worse than Hong Kong!' The second day I went to work as a busboy, and I just wished I had never come to America. I had left all my friends behind in Hong Kong—the big family in the orphanage. And I had come into a new culture with essentially a new family, because I hadn't been with them in all those years. And then to work in a Chinese restaurant as a busboy!"

Today, Dr. Chun Wai Chan speaks eloquently and philosophically of the character-building lessons in self-discipline and perseverance that he had learned in his childhood at the Faith Love Home. But as a 17-year-old in 1968, standing hour after hour over a sink full of dirty dishes in a hot, smelly kitchen in Queens, Chun Wai knew only that he had to change his situation. "The first step," he recalls, "was to find a way to finish high school, since according to the American system I had only completed 11th grade. I called up Information, then I called up the New York City Board of Education, but I didn't know enough English to communicate with them."

Chun Wai received no encouragement or help from his family, who thought that being a busboy (with tips, the job yielded $100 a week) was a very good deal. By Hong Kong standards it was. "The family really didn't want me to go back to school," says Chan, "and my grandfather had his own dream for me. He thought that if I learned enough English, I'd be promoted to waiter and get more tips, and then I might move up to captain, and then manager, and eventually I might even have my own restaurant.

"But from the second day on," says Chan, "I didn't think that would work. I determined instead that the first thing I'd have to do was learn enough English to communicate.

"I listened like mad to the radio; I had it on all the time. Anytime I wasn't doing something else, I was washing dishes, and I'd turn on the radio. I didn't care what I was listening to. I didn't understand what they were talking about anyway, they were talking so fast. I just kept listening, to get used to the tone, to the way they spoke. Gradually I began to understand the weather report. Then some news. And then when I went back to the dorm—at the restaurant I stayed in a dorm—there was an old black-and-white TV that I would turn on. I'd get off from work at one a.m., and the next morning I'd wake up at eight o'clock or so, and I'd turn on 'Sesame Street.' That's how I learned English.

"I had a Chinese-English dictionary, and after the programs I'd memorize all the words from A to Z. I'd memorize word after word. I just kept memorizing and watching 'Sesame Street.' No one taught me, I was doing it all by myself. And then I started practicing on the customers in the restaurant. When I would go to pick up their dishes, I'd strike up a conversation. They liked it. They were very surprised, very supportive of what I was trying to do. So I learned from the customers."

After about three months, Chun Wai again contacted the Board of Education, and using his new command of English, learned that he could go to school. But because he was already 17, he had to enroll in an adult education program. In the adult school an alert student counselor was impressed with the boy's records from Hong Kong and got him admitted to a high school on 18th Street in Manhattan.

In that high school, Chun Wai did extremely well academically. He received extraordinarily high scores on all the exams and placement tests he took—especially in mathematics and the sciences. Another alert school counselor arranged for Chun Wai to take some courses at Brooklyn College while he was still in high school. Although he was concerned about admission to college, he need not have worried. He was admitted to all of the more than half-dozen institutions where he applied. He decided to attend Princeton, where he was offered a full scholarship.

Chun Wai's first year at Princeton was difficult. "I couldn't understand what the professors were talking about! And in my English literature course, of course Shakespeare was difficult even for American students. It was impossible for me." He did so badly that the teacher used to give him two grades, one for content and one for expression. "When the college administration became aware of my difficulties in English," recalls Chan, "they arranged for me to room with a student—an English major—who was willing to drill me in English every day. After a year or so, I had no more problems with English."

At Princeton, Chun Wai did very well academically, and at this point, he realized that his dream of becoming a doctor could be realized. "Until then, I didn't really believe it was possible," he says, his voice still echoing a bit of wonder.

When Chun Wai graduated in 1975, *cum laude,* he entered Harvard Medical School, again on a full scholarship. Dr. Chan completed his internship and his residency in cardiology at the Medical College of Virginia in Richmond. He next moved to Fresno, California, in 1986, and became the chief of cardiology at Kaiser Permanente Hospital. It has been a long, unpredictable journey from the slums of Hong Kong.

How many Chun Wai Chans has CCF produced in more than 50 years of assisting children in a total of 72 countries? Probably not very many, for people like Chan are exceptional. Most of the impact of CCF's work—first in institutions and later in communities—has produced gains in the lives of ordinary people which, though tremendously significant, are difficult to quantify. This is the mainstream of CCF's work. Yet if only one assisted child in a thousand has the talent and potential of a Chun Wai Chan, the value to the world of recognizing and nourishing these special children is incalculable.

In 1979, some months after Chun Wai Chan and his wife (they met as volunteers in a Chinatown health clinic) had moved to Richmond for his internship at the Medical College of Virginia, the couple was invited to attend a Chinese fellowship service in the basement of a local church. The man in the pulpit was preaching in flawless Cantonese Chinese. Impressed, Chan asked someone who the speaker was. "I was told it was a Dr. Mills," he recalls. "The name meant nothing to me. Then I looked at the program. It was bilingual, and the man's Chinese name was familiar to me. He'd gained weight since he was in Hong Kong, and he'd shaved off his mustache, so I hadn't recognized him at all. After he finished preaching, I went up to him and I said, 'Are you the Dr. Mills who was in Hong Kong back in the '50s and '60s?' He replied, 'Probably. Who are you?' And I said, 'I was raised in one of the orphanages in Hong Kong.' We were both very moved, and since then we have become very close."

Now the Chans and the Millses live near each other in Fresno. Chan's oldest daughter is named Alma after Mrs. Mills. His son's name

Dr. and Mrs. Mills in Fresno, California, with family of former CCF child, Dr. Chun Wai Chan of Faith Love Home, Hongkong

is Verent. "Can you imagine that poor little fellow being saddled with a name like Verent?" says Dr. Mills, glowing with pleasure.

Chun Wai Chan was elected a member of CCF's Board of Directors in 1986. He was the first former sponsored child be chosen. This was after he became a sponsor himself in the early 1980s. Today, he sponsors a little girl in Thailand because, he says, "I heard a lot of bad things about the exploitation of little girls there."

Chun Wai Chan's own sponsor, Doris Hawkins, now in a nursing home, speaks of Chun Wai as if he were her own son. It is clear that the biggest events in her life in recent years have been the births of Chun Wai's three children, the second daughter of whom is named after her. "He is the nicest fellow that ever was," she says proudly. "And he's so bright! When he was only a young fellow he wanted to be a doctor. When I think of the little bit of money that I put in for him . . . look at all the blessings he's given to so many people!"

~~~

Kerala, India—1951

In the late 1950s and early 1960s, the Asian and European countries CCF originally assisted began to recover economically and to require less help from abroad. At the same time, voluntary organizations like CCF began to grasp the global dimensions of infant mortality, malnutrition, illiteracy and poverty. In responding to suffering born not of war but of underdevelopment, lack of opportunities and economic exploitation, CCF gradually shifted and broadened its approach in meeting the needs of children. The journey CCF made—from orphanages and schools to "Family Helper" projects and to the purchase of land for cooperatives—was long and labored. Yet each of these various approaches, even those that have been discarded, helped hundreds of thousands of children, and, by extension, *their* children as well. Although the journey was one of gradual evolution and of philosophically changing responses to different problems, CCF's focus on the survival, well-being, and development of children has remained constant.

What changed was an understanding of the causes of the deprivation in which needy children live, and the strategies for lifting them out of that condition. CCF orphanages met the need for shelter, food, and education when war severed children from their homes and families. CCF boarding schools removed children from squalid living conditions, economic servitude, and social disenfranchisement and offered them opportunities their illiterate parents could not provide. Yet, while individual children benefited immensely from schools, the overall poverty of their families changed little. But the seeds of a different approach were already coming to fruition.

In 1927, Lester Williams Hooper, an English missionary traveling in South India, described in the emotionally charged language of his day the socioeconomic deprivation he observed in the princely state of Travancore. Ironically, this lush, densely populated coastal state (re-named Kerala, "land of coconuts," after Indian independence) had a literacy rate of 90 percent at the time, and today leads India as a model of social development. Yet the socioeconomic conditions Hooper observed among the low-caste "untouchables" of the region moved him to exclaim: "I have never seen such wrecks of humanity in God's family, such absolute starvation of body and soul. They are the victims of everything devilish with a big 'D,' dirt, debt, drink, drugs, disease, despair, destitution, degradation, demon worship."

To improve the lot of such unfortunates, Mr. Hooper founded a school in a village called Alwaye. It was designed primarily for untouchable children whose families had converted to Christianity. Kerala's population is 30 percent Christian and has long had the largest proportion of Christians among the states of India. When the British government relinquished its control of India in 1947, however, English funds for church-supported schools like Alwaye began to dry up. When the Rev. Erwin Raetz learned of the school's difficulties in 1951, he suggested that CCF come to the rescue. For the next 20 years, CCF's involvement with the Alwaye Settlement School was typical of the agency's school-based activities throughout the period.

The setting of the Alwaye School is magically beautiful. Although tropically hot and humid throughout the year, it is refreshed by breezes sweeping inland from the Indian Ocean. Brilliant green vegetation is everywhere. Rice paddies glisten like thick, velvet carpets, and the shiny fronds of coconut palms sway and rattle in the bright yellow sunlight. In the verdant village of Alwaye, the Settlement School rises like a fortress of middle-class stability on its gently sloping hill. The tan stucco buildings with dark red shutters and trim, which CCF built in the 1950s, are sturdy, spacious and attractive in an old-fashioned, colonial sort of way. Even in 1990, amid the relative prosperity of modern Kerala, the Alwaye School was still the most imposing and substantial structure for miles around.

During the CCF years, Alwaye Settlement was a boarding school for poor children, 70 percent of whom came from the untouchable caste. When CCF took over there were only 30 students; when CCF finished its work in 1972, there were 300. During CCF's tenure only orphans and one-parent children were admitted, thus ensuring that opportunities for an entirely new life—in a sense, even a new identity—would be offered to the most deprived children in the area.

The Alwaye Settlement Annual for 1964, most of which is printed in the ornate script of Malayalam, the local language, mimics similar yearbooks published at that time by English boarding schools thousands of miles away. Photographs of Dr. and Mrs. J. Calvitt Clarke are prominently reproduced near the front. Other photos record School Day celebrations, the drama club—with actors in costume and "white face"—the football team, the crafts class, and rows of tidy, demure young ladies in white dresses from the Girls' Home. Clearly, the Alwaye School did not leave Hooper's "wrecks of humanity" where they were found.

"We wanted the children to be able to get a decent living, a good house and income, so we educated them for this," says A.C. John, a gentle, warmhearted man who was business manager of Alwaye during the 1960s. Spiritual education was also emphasized, and the children were encouraged to be active in the church. "We also wanted to help the children develop their personalities," says Mr. John, "and for this we encouraged arts and sports. Our goal was that in every field of life they should shine! They had a contribution to make to the community. They became leaders in their communities and the church because of their good education, even though they were outcasts and were at first accepted in society with reluctance."

Cherakalakudiyil Ulhannan, who simply calls himself C.U., was born in 1956 in a village of mud huts not far from Cochin, the ancient port city of the region, known for centuries to spice traders as the Malabar coast. C.U. was the youngest of six children. His mother, an agricultural day laborer, died of tuberculosis when he was two. His father, also a field hand, earned 10 rupees a day (about 60 cents in 1990), but his health was poor. In any case, work was often simply unavailable—a common problem in India with its huge unskilled labor force.

"My parents were illiterate," says C.U. "My father was not very keen on education. There was no motive; what was the point? Just supporting us was a real problem, and going to school required clothing, books, a lot of expense. When I went to school I went without lunch, and in the morning I just had some rice. Proper food was not available." At age 11, C.U. was about to be taken out of the fifth grade in his village school and sent to work on a local farm, just like his brothers before him. But it so happened that a relative was studying at the Alwaye Settlement School, and somehow C.U. was admitted.

In the school's records there are two sheets of paper labeled "Adoption Assignment" and dated 1967 and 1968. A small black and white photograph of the young C.U. is stapled to the upper right-hand corner of each. These are file copies of the documents the child's sponsors, a couple from Harmony, Minnesota, received for those years. The 1967 photo depicts an eager little face with a toothy grin, black hair slicked back and parted in the middle. C.U. wore a pristine white shirt. Various facts pertaining to the child are recorded on the paper. C.U.'s health is decribed as "poor but improving," and he is characterized as "friendly, hardworking, gentle," an assessment still apt. In the 1968 photo, the smile is still toothy, but more confident. The hair has been allowed to assume its natural waves. C.U.'s health is still "poor but improving," but by 1968 he had become "friendly, hardworking, and energetic." On both sheets "arithmetic" is cited as the boy's favorite subject. Initially, his school chores consisted of "picking up leaves from the yard." Later, he graduated to "cleaning the chapel."

Today, C.U. is a charming, sophisticated, personable young man with a mustache, well-tailored clothes and a Seiko watch. He speaks exceptionally good English, delivered in the special, lilting, rhythmic way of Indians. He drives a motor scooter and has three different business cards, one for each of his ventures as exclusive South Indian sales representative for three different manufacturing firms. C.U.'s manner is relaxed and confident. It is clear that he would be comfortable in virtually any setting anywhere in the world. He may have been born one of the poorest of the world's poor, but today C.U. can only be described as that rare, yet increasingly common phenomenon: a young, Indian, upwardly mobile professional.

If it were not for the Alwaye School, he would be a rubber-tapper or a day laborer, as was his father before him. "I am in this situation today just because I got that opportunity," he says. "That is 100 percent sure. I was about to stop my education and go for small work at home."

C.U. remembers his years at Alwaye as "a beautiful time. It was totally like heaven at the Settlement. Everybody was kind to me, we were fed regularly, we played. The academic standard was slightly above average," he adds with the wisdom of hindsight. But what C.U. recalls most vividly was the contrast between his family's home life and the new and totally different world of his beautiful school. "When I went home I had to work, taking care of the goats and things like that," he says. "My house was totally made of clay with a palm roof, and in the monsoon season it used to collapse and we would have to move. When I came to the school it was like a palace to me."

C.U. went on to study chemistry at Agra University, one of India's finest, far to the north in the Mogul city famous for the Taj Mahal. He planned to be a university lecturer, simply because, he says, the teachers at Alwaye were his only role models—the only educated professionals he had ever known. Instead, he was offered a job in business at almost three times the salary of an academic and he was soon on his way to a business career. Today C.U. supports his wife and child, a sister, a brother and the brother's family. He also contributes to the families of his other brothers—all day laborers—in times of need. "We do it happily," he says, reflecting a traditional sense of Indian familial obligation. "Now that everything is going smoothly for me, I cannot see them suffering." As a successful businessman, C.U. has an annual income greater than that of 90 percent of his 844 million countrymen. He is unquestionably the first member of his family ever to have achieved such prosperity.

Through the years, C.U. has remained especially close to his American former sponsors. They began their letters to him, "My Dear Son." He even put off his wedding for two years until the couple from Minnesota had saved up the money to come to India and attend the ceremony.

Like Dr. Chun Wai Chan, C.U. is a highly intelligent and gifted individual: an outstanding beneficiary of CCF sponsorship. Few graduates of the Alwaye Settlement School, it is safe to say, have done as well materially as he. Indeed, for the average CCF child, the impact of sponsorship may seem comparatively small: freedom from hunger, an adequate place to live, an education and access to a livelihood. Yet these advantages are monumental, and their ripple effect is tremendous—especially in a country where members of extended families with any income at all usually support relatives less fortunate than themselves. Furthermore, the impact of CCF's work is considerable because its children have usually been drawn from the poorest of families, those who would have virtually no other opportunities for receiving an education and improving their economic status. This is particularly true in India, where—despite legislation and affirmative action programs—the caste system continues to bar millions from rising out of abject poverty. The parents of most Alwaye students in the 1950s and 1960s were among the poorest of the poor, low-caste, illiterate day laborers like C.U.'s father. Today, a random sampling of Alwaye alumni from the same period reveals an employee of a business firm, two teachers, a civil servant, two drivers, a day care worker, a tailor, an accountant, a mechanical supervisor and an industrialist who manufactures microinstruments and who himself today assists four needy children at the Alwaye School.

After twenty years of being nurtured by CCF, the school, in 1972, felt it was ready for independence. CCF and school administrators thought the institution could become self-sufficient by marketing the products of its dairy farm and coconut and rubber plantations. It was hoped that profits would be sufficient to maintain an extensive tuition-free program. That plan, however, did not succeed, even though the rubber business continues on a small scale. Today, the Alwaye School still swarms with shiny-haired, bright-eyed students: boys in maroon trousers or shorts and crisp white shirts, girls in mid-calf maroon skirts and immaculate white blouses. But the school has had to rely on tuition for much of its income. Most of the beautiful children and teenagers who whisper in clutches in the dusty schoolyard or recite in unison in their spartan, high-ceilinged classrooms—90 percent of them, to be precise—are from the local middle class whose families are able to pay the stiff tuition fee to attend.

On the back of the hill where the school buildings stand is a long, low house with a shady veranda. Through the windows, one sees rows of small iron beds with chests of drawers beside them. In the old days, this is where the boarders—poor children like C.U.—used to live. Today, out of 580 students there are only ten boarders.

But there are other measures of the changed circumstances. There are fewer of Mr. Hooper's "wrecks of humanity" in Kerala today, thanks, in part, to institutions like the Alwaye School. Assistance to a Family Helper project started in a nearby village in 1966 was also discontinued in May of 1990, when the entire state of Kerala was judged to have become too prosperous—relative to other Indian states—to require further help.

~~~

During the 1950s CCF learned that the housing, clothing, and feeding of homeless children were not enough. If CCF was to be an effective force in the world of children, it had to find ways of assisting children outside the confines of orphanages. That was done marvelously in Hong Kong in the early 1950s and then in India in the same decade. By the late 1950s CCF was hard at work providing basic educational opportunities for all of its assisted children. Whether the school was operated by CCF or received assistance from CCF, every child had the benefit of acquiring a rudimentary education. CCF's commitment to education came early in its career and has remained a central feature of its programs to the present.

Chapter Four

FROM "ADOPTION" TO FAMILY ASSISTANCE, 1953-1970

J. Calvitt Clarke's dream of an international child "adoption" agency able to intervene in the war zones of the world achieved its greatest pinnacle of success in the late 1950s. And along with success came no small amount of fame for the founder of what was China's Children Fund, but which had later become the widely known Christian Children's Fund. Everywhere Clarke turned there was recognition for his brilliant achievements.

The Universal-International Pictures release of *Battle Hymn* in 1956 telling the story of Colonel Dean Hess's dramatic rescue of CCF's Korean children touched hearts throughout the world. The publication of John C. Caldwell's popular *Children of Calamity* in 1957 detailing his visits to CCF projects in fifteen countries and describing CCF's inspiring work added abundantly to the mystique of Clarke and his band of faithful sponsors.

And, then, there were the awards and ceremonies. In the spring of 1957, Dr. and Mrs. Clarke were received by the Emperor and Empress of Japan in the Royal Palace and congratulated for the contributions of CCF to the recovery of Japan. In 1958 they got the same treatment from Madame Chiang Kai-shek at the Presidential Residence in Taiwan for CCF's many contributions both there and on the mainland. In Korea, during the same visit, President Syngman Rhee presented Clarke with a Ribbon of Honor for CCF's work in that recovering nation.

The string of honors just kept on coming, especially from these grateful nations. In 1961, the Emperor of Japan entered Clarke into the

Fourth Class of the Order of the Sacred Treasure at special ceremonies held at the Japanese Consulate in New York. Not to be outdistanced, Chiang Kai-shek then inducted Clarke into the Chinese Order of the Brilliant Star and Korean officials put him into the Order of Cultural Merit.[1]

The crowning touch, however, came in 1961 with the publication of a book titled *Yankee Si!* with a reverential subtitle, *The Story of Dr. J. Calvitt Clarke and His 36,000 Children*. The book was written by Edmund W. Janss, staff director of research for CCF. With a stirring foreword written by author and lecturer Daniel A. Poling, the book was published by William Morrow & Company of New York in sufficient quantity to be sent to every CCF sponsor. Also issued in an inexpensive 142-page paper format by the Popular Library of New York, the little book could be purchased on newsstands for only fifty cents. Complete with a picture of the friendly, grandfatherly Clarke on the back cover, *Yankee Si!* made Clarke a household figure to millions of Americans.

What more could a man at age 74 want out of life! Honor and glory throughout the world, beloved by the thousands of sponsors who faithfully sent $10 a month in 1961 for the benefit of their "adopted" child, and venerated by a worldwide staff and 36,000 "adopted" children. This had to be a time of great satisfaction and fulfillment for both of the Clarkes.

And yet, just two years later, the Clarkes would be severed from their relationship with their beloved organization. They would be so hurt in the process that they would found a whole new organization to care for children. And, to add final insult to injury, CCF would reissue *Yankee Si!* in 1967 in a slightly expanded and revised version under the title *A Brief History of Christian Children's Fund, Inc.*, with every single reference to either Calvitt or Helen Clarke deleted! Wherever the Clarke name had once appeared, the revised version said either "director" or "CCF."[2]

What brought about this sad circumstance was almost predictable in an organization like Christian Children's Fund. It was an agency created and nurtured by two devoted souls who could not let it go, who would not let it change, and who perhaps thought it could not survive without them. Add to these factors the further reality that CCF had

---

[1] All of the special honors and awards mentioned here are detailed in Janss, *Yankee Si!*, pp. 10-12, 65 (paper edition).

[2] The revision was issued directly by CCF. One can easily follow the textual changes since a typist actually physically deleted the Clarke name and typed in revisions on the master copy!

become a powerful force in the world affecting many lives in more than 50 nations, necessitating change to enable the organization to maintain its vitality. Even as Clarke received his great honors, the need for change was evident. All that was missing was the means and the timing.

~~~

Seoul, Korea—1953

By 1952 CCF's operations in Korea had become so extensive and complex that they could no longer be administered from a remote office in Hong Kong on a part-time basis. A national office just for Korea was needed and one that could respond to the changing needs of the thousands of children under CCF's care. A Korean, Dr. Roe Chin Pak, was appointed field representative in Korea, but after a short time, he became ill and died. In 1953, a Canadian was sent out to set up a CCF office in Pusan. Then, in 1954, two young Mennonites from the United States boarded a steamer in Seattle bound for Korea. One of them was James C. Hostetler from Louisville, Ohio.

"I was of draft age," says Hostetler, later CCF's regional coordinator for Asia and then for Eastern Europe. "Being a Mennonite and a conscientious objector, I chose not to be part of the military establishment." At that time, alternate service for conscientious objectors usually involved working in mental hospitals in the U.S., but overseas relief work was also available. With the Mennonite Central Committee acting as a placement service, young Hostetler asked to be assigned to a relief agency in the Orient. His first choice was Japan; his second was Taiwan. But he was offered a job as an accountant attached to CCF's Korean operation.

And he was not alone. The time had come to improve child care in all of CCF's Korean orphanages. As a result, another Mennonite, Helen Tieszen, instructor in early childhood development at the University of Iowa, found herself on that same steamer headed for Korea. According to Hostetler, the need for such a person was acute.

"CCF had all these orphanages that we were helping, and the children were coming in at age three and four and five, and conditions were so bad. Sometimes the children were just herded into temples or churches or school buildings and someone would come along and say, 'This is an orphanage and I'm the director.' Often it was the strong, aggressive types who became the directors of these overnight orphanages."

American soldiers often gave the "directors" what in Korea were large sums of money. The more children they could cram into a home,

Dr. Calvitt Clarke and Helen Clarke receiving the Ribbon of Honor from President Syngman Rhee of South Korea, 1958

the more money they would receive. Proper care, or even humane treatment of the children, was often not a high priority, Hostetler recalls.

For the most part, this type of "upstart" orphanage did not become associated with international organizations like CCF. But in these years, even when CCF agreed to assist institutions run by foreign missionaries, the number of children who could be accommodated was often a more pressing issue than the quality of care provided. With the arrival of Tieszen, however, the latest concepts of child psychology and development began to be applied to the war-battered, hunger-hardened children of Korea.

She trained the orphanage personnel—including the house mothers at Dr. Oh's cottage-plan orphanage—in advanced methods of child care, and also worked with the children herself. Or rather, she played, and she taught the other staff members to do the same. Children, who before had only snatched moments of play from the tension and insecurity of their daily struggle to survive, were now playing in peaceful, supportive, supervised settings for the first time. Tieszen worked with puppets, using the children's responses to make-believe situations to assess their feelings and emotional health. "Some of the

Koreans couldn't believe that this woman had come all the way from America to watch children play," says Jim Hostetler, "but she helped them understand what they were doing to the children, and she was able to show that her approach produced results." Helen Tieszen remained with CCF for the next three years. Later she served as director of the Child Development Research Institute at Yonsei University in Seoul.

The arrival of Helen Tieszen marked the beginning of CCF's transformation into a professional organization with carefully conceived, consistent child care policies. From being an informal "homemade" charity, CCF was becoming a well-run international agency with a defined mission and philosophy.

In the mid-fifties, CCF's Seoul office staff consisted of three foreigners and seven Koreans. One of the Koreans, Chung Ii Sook, went on to become a member of the board of directors of Korea Children's Foundation, CCF's Korean counterpart organization. Today she is chairman of the board of Ewha Woman's University in Seoul, the world's largest university for women, and formerly served as its president.

Over the years, CCF has provided employment opportunities to countless nationals in more than 60 countries around the world. In 1990 CCF employed, directly and indirectly, more than 5,000 people in its 24 national offices and 1,453 projects, and 200 people in its Richmond headquarters. Throughout the world, CCF policy favors the employment of nationals of the countries in which CCF projects are located in virtually all positions, including managerial posts. This is a vast change from the 1950s, when the agency relied almost entirely on Westerners, primarily American, Canadian or British missionaries.

By 1955, CCF was a major international force, assisting hundreds of orphanages and schools in 15 Asian countries with an annual budget of $1,811,127.50. Nevertheless, despite a growing sophistication in the hands-on execution of its activities, CCF still regarded itself as a charitable organization whose primary function was the distribution of money for the benefit of children. "When you put money that comes from outside the country into the hands of missionaries," says James Hostetler today, "they tend to become 'great white fathers' in the eyes of the recipients." This fostered and perpetuated a well-meaning but wrongheaded paternalistic relationship between CCF-assisted institutions and the children they served. "We had the image of being a paternalistic kind of agency," he says. "It took us a long time to break away from that."

At its peak in the late 1950s, CCF was assisting more than 38,000 children in 72 orphanages in Korea. Planning, professional expertise,

A "family helper" worker meeting with a prospective CCF family in Taiwan, 1965

and hard work had improved the quality of child care in the institutions, and the results were gratifying. The children were well housed, well fed, and were receiving an education. They were "graduating" from the institutions with the skills they would need to get good jobs and become responsible citizens: CCF was justifiably proud of the contribution it was making to the rebuilding of a nation.

But then a new problem emerged: many of the children in CCF orphanages were suddenly no longer orphans. The Korean Association of Voluntary Agencies, known as KAVA, conducted a study in 1960 to determine where the children in the CCF-assisted institutions had come from, how long they had been in the homes, and how many of them actually returned to their families when they left. The findings were unequivocal. A large proportion of these children had been transformed into "orphans" by their families. "We began to understand that by working exclusively in institutional settings," says Hostetler, "we were were actually *bringing* children into institutions. Parents would go through all kinds of shenanigans to get their child into an orphanage so that he could get an education."

After much study and soul-searching, CCF decided that in Korea, it would divert at least part of its resources to helping children within their own families. The Korean staff was aided in making this move into unknown territory by a group of university graduates from the new school of social work that had recently been founded with American assistance at Seoul National University. Helen Tieszen also played a major role in designing the very first of what CCF still calls its "Family Helper Projects."

The new approach was a major departure for CCF. Yet the agency has continued to evolve so far from where it was in 1960, that today Jim Hostetler is bemused when he recalls that first Family Helper Project. "It was like an AFDC [Aid to Families with Dependent Children] program in this country," he says. "In our innocence—and probably ignorance—we used the 'casework' method as a way to help the children.

"The emphasis was on what *we* could do for *them*. There was little thought of encouraging people to do something for themselves. We did not understand that in order to maximize our resources, the best thing would have been to get these people working together from the start. They were capable of doing that, but somehow we saw them as 'cases.' We had caseworkers," he says with another wry chuckle. "They would go out and deliver the money to the families. There was very little interaction between the families."

CCF programs involving individual families were soon established in Taiwan, and later in Brazil. Other agencies, such as World Vision and

Compassion, eventually followed CCF's lead. But Jim Hostetler now decries CCF's early "caseworker" approach to development. "The assumption," he says, "is that the beneficiary—a young mother, for example—can't make decisions for herself; that she needs a caseworker to get approval from if she wants to spend money for this or for that." The caseworker approach assumes that the individuals and families being aided are dysfunctional.

"In those days, we did not realize that what people need most is control over their own lives," says Hostetler. "In most cases, it is the absence of such control that causes dysfunction. In Korea in the late 1950s and early 1960s," he explains, "the real need was very specific— funds to enable children to get an education. There were not a lot of social problems to justify the intervention of caseworkers.

In shifting its efforts in Korea to Family Helper programs, CCF responded to the needs of the day, and set a pattern that would benefit hundreds of thousands of children throughout the world in the years ahead. Originally the agency had been founded to rescue children from the ravages of war. By the 1960s it was beginning to understand that another kind of violence—less obvious perhaps, but no less brutal— was at work. Over the next decades, in scores of countries on every continent, economic forces would prove to be every bit as destructive to the well-being of children as the Japanese invasion of China or the Korean War had been.

~~~

Richmond, Virginia—1963

The early 1950s were years of rapid growth for Christian Children's Fund. With orphanages and schools in nearly 70 countries, the agency's assistance of destitute children through sponsorship had reached all the trouble spots and recovering war zones of Asia, the Middle East, and Europe. So many children were being sponsored, housed, fed, and educated, it seemed, that there could not possibly still be more to assist.

"We thought that by ten years after the Second World War, we would have met all the needs of the children in the world," says Verent Mills a bit ruefully, "and that we wouldn't have to function any more. That was our concept then, because we believed that the problem of children in need was due exclusively to the destruction and privations of war.

"But our education was just beginning. That was when we began to learn about the Third World and its needs—South America and so on—whole areas of terrific need."

CCF was just starting to realize the intractable scope of the world's problems. There is now, four decades later, worldwide recognition that hundreds of millions of people—the majority of them children—live in unacceptable conditions of poverty. And there are persistent, concerted, large-scale efforts to change these conditions. But in the 1950s the idea that the world's poor don't *choose* to live the way they do was to many a novel one. So too was the notion that poverty should be eliminated and that, collectively, we have a moral obligation to do so. Today, the absolute number of people touched by poverty is greater than it was 30 years ago. The crucial difference is that fewer people assume that widespread poverty is an irreducible, even necessary, part of the human condition.

After almost 30 years of laboring for the welfare of children in China, Korea, and Japan, Verent Mills was transferred from Hong Kong to CCF's home office in Richmond. The move for Mills and his family was emotional since his heart and home were rooted in Asia and he was immensely proud of his work there as CCF's overseas director. However, CCF was in the midst of a fundamental redirection. New leaders were coming to the helm, on CCF's board of directors and among the staff, who wanted the organization to get out of the orphanage and real estate business and to find other means of achieving its ambitious world mission.

In one of those zigzags experienced in the life of every vibrant institution, CCF's directors began to question the wisdom of expending its funds on capital improvements—especially ones as expensive to build and maintain as those for Mills' prized Children's Garden orphanage in Hong Kong. Whereas just a few years before such a model development was viewed as a laudable achievement in a world teeming with needy children, it became clear that CCF needed to develop less intensive and less costly, but effective, forms of assistance to the largest possible number of children.

As CCF's Overseas Director based in Hong Kong, Mills had traveled the globe, visiting CCF-assisted orphanages and schools from Korea to Italy and from Lebanon to Finland. During this period, except in pilot Korean Family Helper projects, CCF children were being cared for in institutions, away from their families. Yet, at Mills' insistence, many of the institutions attempted to provide a semblance of home life. Certainly, this was true of those designed on the cottage plan, where a group of children in the care of a "housemother" re-created, as far as possible, a family setting. Indeed, it was assumed that the homes and projects under Dr. Mills' periodic scrutiny, were assuring that sponsored children were being housed, fed, clothed and educated.

Ironically, despite CCF's extraordinary success (by 1960, the annual budget had risen to more than $4.5 million), little, if any, specific guidance emanated from headquarters in Richmond concerning the philosophical basis of the organization's hands-on operations in the field. During the 1950s and 1960s, there was no one on the staff in Richmond responsible for defining and directing CCF's actual work with children overseas.

Although CCF's programs worked amazingly well, little attention had been spent to date analyzing the most effective way of assisting growing numbers of children. Suddenly a series of events conspired to transform CCF from a society for the adoption of distressed children into a very sophisticated development agency.

Verbon E. Kemp, 2nd CCF Executive Director, 1964-1970

The changes were brought about partly by changing world needs. But they were also wrought by the need for CCF to find a system of leadership succession. By 1963 Dr. J. Calvitt Clarke, patron father of CCF, was 76 years of age. He and Mrs. Clarke increasingly focused on that part of CCF's work they most enjoyed—the recruitment and nurturing of sponsors and the collection of funds to save the deprived children of the world. As the world of charitable organizations changed and as world sociopolitical forces brought increasing poverty to the Third World, CCF needed to adopt new programs and standards expected of international assistance agencies.

The need for change and the means of change converged when CCF's public relations director Jerald Huntsinger, a former journalist from Kansas, threatened to publish an article critical of the Clarkes and their outmoded style of operation. Rightly or wrongly, Huntsinger's challenge ushered in a season of transition. "I had no personal animosity toward the Clarkes," Huntsinger said, "but they *were* the organization, and the time had come for the organization to be separate from the Clarke family."

Huntsinger's complaints soon permeated the entire organization and got the attention of CCF's board of directors. The board was comprised of some of Richmond's most eminent citizens: among these were two former mayors of Richmond, two members of the City

Council, the executive director of the Virginia State Chamber of Commerce, two members of the Virginia State Corporation Commission, and the Chief Justice of the Supreme Court of Virginia.

"We had people of stature on the board," says Jim Hostetler. They did not want to preside over an organization that was outmoded or failing to achieve its highest goals. They, therefore, suggested to the Clarkes that a time for change had arrived. On December 10, 1963, 25 years after founding CCF, Dr. and Mrs. Clarke tendered their resignations. The board, with "a glowing tribute to their dedicated service, and with sincere regrets and admiration," accepted.

In a somewhat odd move at a time of critical transition, the secretary of the board, Verbon Kemp, executive director of the Virginia State Chamber of Commerce, was named the new International Director of Christian Children's Fund. An old friend of the Clarkes, Kemp, to the surprise of most observers, decided to make radical changes at CCF. First of all, he isolated Dr. and Mrs. Clarke, who were cherishing their emeritus status, from the central operations of CCF. Some of the CCF faithful chafed at this bypassing of the founders. But then Kemp also took steps to professionalize CCF in a manner never before conceived. He hired staff with degrees in development and child care. Never had such folk been involved in CCF planning and operations.

The Clarkes, in the process, felt that Kemp had pushed them aside, perhaps unfairly. They had been grooming their daughter, Jeanne, to take over CCF when they retired. Hence, when Kemp and the CCF board headed in a direction different from their ideas, they chose to establish a new sponsorship agency with daughter Jeanne at the helm. In the process, they took the names and addresses of the CCF sponsors with them—a list of tens of thousands of names—hoping to transfer them to their new organization.

They were greatly disappointed when few of the old sponsors chose to join them in the new venture. Children, Incorporated, it is called and the Clarkes' daughter, Jeanne Clarke Wood, administers it from her home in Richmond to the present day. Interestingly, Children, Incorporated, with its practice of working exclusively through missionaries and church institutions, closely resembles the CCF of the 1940s and 1950s. In a real sense it is a memorial to the creative work of the Clarkes during the central decades of the twentieth century. Although J. Calvitt Clarke was isolated from his greatest monument when he died in 1970, no one failed to recognize his great achievement in founding and building up CCF. Clarke died at the age of 83, three years after Helen's death.

Jerald Huntsinger, instigator of this essential transition, attributes CCF's emergence as a modern, sophisticated, fiscally responsible development organization in large part to the energy, professionalism, and vision of the Clarkes' successor, Verbon Kemp (1900-1981). "If anyone was a hero [in the transition], it was Kemp," he says. "Kemp made the [CCF] board an active, participating body with social welfare expertise. And he brought a new version of business management techniques to CCF. He equipped CCF to deal with the realities and complexities of the modern world. It was a critical period for the organization." Kemp served as director of CCF from 1964 until 1970.

Between 1965 and 1970, while CCF was being transformed by Kemp, Verent Mills was appointed to a succession of different jobs within the organization: regional director, overseas director, coordinator, and director of operations. He remembers how Kemp tackled another realm of CCF's work badly in need of renovation: recordkeeping and financial controls. Crucial changes were made during those years. "At that time, everything was done manually, and there was a very high error factor," says Mills. "We had maybe 200 people in the office, and they were typing receipts to send to the sponsors. Often, they were months behind in this work, and the recordkeeping was pretty hit-or-miss.

"We bought two more buildings, one on either side of the original one at 108 South Third Street, and punched holes through the walls to join the three. Then we started putting in computers and quality control." Naturally, the advent of computers meant that many of the clerical workers would be made redundant, but it was decided that staff reduction would be accomplished through attrition. "During the transition to computers," says Mills, "the staff was reduced from 200 to 140 without firing anyone."

It soon became apparent that three townhouses were not adequate for a large and growing organization. "They were typical three-story brick Virginia homes—not offices," says Mills. There were no elevators and the stairs were steep and potentially hazardous. The space was cramped. So in 1965, again under Kemp's leadership, a rather sterile, two-story office building that was to house CCF until 1991 was completed. Wills and bequests and other reserve funds, not sponsorship money, financed its construction.

By the time Verbon Kemp retired in 1970, a system of financial controls had been put in place which greatly improved CCF's ability to ensure that sponsorship funds were being properly used by the hundreds of affiliated projects around the world. He was also responsible for two other major innovations during this period—regular program audits and the inclusion of child welfare experts on the board of directors. Over the years, both have contributed significantly to CCF's effectiveness and credibility.

~~~

Belo Horizonte, Brazil—1964

CCF's original, institutional child welfare system had evolved in response to the chaotic wartime and post-war conditions in East Asia, when thousands of orphans and other children had been separated from their families and needed immediate care. As the system evolved and spread, the sponsored child who was cared for in an institution such as the Alwaye School in Kerala, India, was inevitably singled out as the favored one in his or her family. Not only did other family members receive few or no benefits, but a gulf often grew between the one child who was able to better himself and his sometimes jealous siblings who remained mired in conditions of poverty. Chun Wai Chan from Hong Kong speaks sadly of the alienation he felt from his siblings during the years he was growing up at Faith Love Orphanage.

But in most Family Helper projects of the 1960s and 1970s, *all* the children in a family—and today, all the children in a community—are enrolled in CCF projects and receive benefits such as access to education and nutritious food. The children's parents are also assisted in increasing their income, and the family's overall living conditions are improved. Today, the only thing that sets sponsored children apart is interaction with their sponsors; the only material benefits sponsored children receive which their siblings do not are the gifts of money sent by many sponsors for birthdays, Christmas or other occasions. In fact, sponsors often request that these gifts be used to buy needed clothes or other items for brothers and sisters as well as for the sponsored child.

CCF has transformed itself quite consciously from an organization promoting symbolic "adoptions" of a single child by an individual sponsor to an agent of whole community development. "Our policy is to enroll every eligible family in a project area," says David Herrell, CCF's director of child and family services from 1973 to 1990, "and this certainly democratizes the system. But it's still not perfect. Sometimes there is a dilemma about which child or children in a family receive formal schooling if, for a number of reasons, it is not possible to provide such education to all the children in the family. In this situation, the selection responsibility lies at the local project level. Sometimes we find that they tend to choose the boys rather than the girls, and we come in with some stronger guidelines and quotas. We've had to do this in India, for example."

Today, CCF focuses not only on the child and the family, but on the community as well. Today, sponsorship money is made to go further and benefit more children than in the past by pooling resources at the community level and helping children and their families on a community wide basis. In the Family Helper projects of the 1960s, when sponsorship funds were channeled directly to each family, the agency sponsored as many children under age 12 in each family as possible. "This is what kept families together," asserts Verent Mills. "Just one sponsorship was never enough to keep the family going. We may not have been able to sponsor all the children in each family, but we'd help two or three, and as interest grew here at home and more sponsors signed on, we would increase the number."

CCF's practice of channeling funds to help whole families is a step away from charity toward community development. But explaining the merits of this approach to sponsors is difficult for CCF and its International Partnership Organizations around the world. For example, Robert Brooks, the National Director of Christian Children's Fund of Australia, has strong views about the challenge of "selling" CCF to potential sponsors. In his promotional work with the Australian public, he still prefers to emphasize the "charity" aspect of CCF's work.

"For most people, the primary benefit of sponsorship is a nice warm feeling inside that they're doing something to help another person—a child whose name they know—who's less well off than they are," says Mr. Brooks in his friendly Australian twang. "That is the focus of our advertising. We appeal to the people's emotional side, not their rational side. Very few people make the decision in rational terms that they have X dollars and these children have so much less, and it's the correct thing to do to give X percent of their income to the less well-off people in the world."

Brooks endorses the concept of community-based projects and agrees that this is the most efficient and productive use of sponsorship funds. While he is troubled that sponsors may occasionally misunderstand the way CCF works, he contends that marketing the concept of child sponsorship is a very effective method of raising funds, precisely because of the emotional relationship between the sponsor and the child. "Community development is a better way of helping people," he says, "but that's not something people are moved to give money for; it doesn't give them an emotional reward. Whereas they are rewarded emotionally by helping an individual child."

Although it is true that CCF sponsorship funds are used to benefit the sponsored child's entire community, the quality of the sponsorship relationship and its impact on the individual child need not be diluted by this sharing of resources. What establishes the relationship is communication on the sponsor's part. In the cases where sponsors write to their sponsored child on a regular basis, the "warm feeling" Brooks speaks of can be very strong on both sides, and develops irrespective of how the sponsorship funds are allocated. It is the letters from sponsors that the children value most—even more than the additional gifts of money their sponsors occasionally send. A relationship built on communication feeds the entire family's self-esteem and gives them a sense of equality with their benefactor.

When it comes to explaining CCF's philosophy, Naval Dave, Director of the North Indian National Office in New Delhi, is one of the agency's most eloquent and persuasive spokesmen. "If you want a child to grow, you must create conditions wherein children have the possibility of growing," says this former professor of social sciences. "And when you are creating such conditions, you are not concerned with only one child. Children's health, education, and survival have to be taken care of. At the same time, part of the available resources must be used in a way that helps families to provide for their children's needs. This can range from making safe drinking water available, to improving the land by providing irrigation facilities, or even to growing a forest if necessary."

This kind of comprehensive approach to improving the lives of children was not fully implemented by CCF until the 1980s. But already in the mid-1960s the basis for such an approach, the Family Helper projects, was becoming more widespread. Such projects in Brazil "caught fire" in no time, Verent Mills says, not only in Rio de Janeiro, but also in Belo Horizonte, where CCF's first South American office was opened in 1964. "When I saw all these families living on the mountainside outside of Belo Horizonte—refugees from the interior— I knew that the Family Helper program would be the thing for them," says Mills.

At the heart of these Family Helper projects in the 1960s was a center of social services, with a supervisor, caseworkers, and a place for a library, classrooms, and often a recreation center as well. "At first we didn't have professional caseworkers going into the homes," Mills recalls. "We had what we called 'social visitors.' They were high school graduates—often girls, but boys as well—who were interested in social work and were in the midst of training as well as doing this work. They would start out by going to a home to visit with the mother.

"'What does your hubby do?' they would ask.

"'He's unemployed.'

"'How many children have you?'

"'Six.'

"'They going to school?'

"'Nope.'

"'What do you do for a living?'

"'I sew whenever I can. I go out and work. My husband tries to get work wherever he can.'

"So the social visitor got a case report of the family, where they came from, how long they'd been there. Then she'd go back and tell them, 'Look, we're going to organize this project. All those who want to participate in it can do so. We will sponsor the children with so much money to help you buy your groceries, and help you with your home. But every child of school age, five years and older, must go to school. If you don't send your children to school, we will not help you.'"

The mothers came to the center during the day, or sometimes at night, to attend classes in nutrition, literacy, budgeting, sewing. Sewing machines were available to help them learn to sew. At first, sponsorship money was not given directly to the mothers. Instead, the national office set up a cooperative where the mothers could buy rice, beans, manioc and other staples which were distributed by weight according to the number of children in each family. And, volunteer doctors came to the center to give the children inoculations.

Initially, most of the sponsorship money was spent on food. But as the projects grew and funds increased, money became available for education, clothing, and medical and dental care.

"Gradually we improved the program," says Mills, "and after a while, part of the sponsorship money for each project was deposited in the bank. The mothers had to take their subsidy check for their monthly subsidy and deposit it. They had their own little savings accounts. If they wanted to withdraw money, they had to take their bank deposit book to do it."

At this point, the mothers themselves decided to form a cooperative which would enable them to borrow money for emergencies or to start their own small businesses. They each contributed a small amount—about $2—every month to the fund.

"There may have been a few who just lived off the subsidy money as a handout," Mills admits. "But for most, involvement with CCF meant a lot more than material help. The social visitor went three times a month to the home, to check on how the children were doing, how things were going in the home, and whether or not the parents were participating in the project. Then, of course, once the children were going to school, they could come to the project center to do their homework, and the social visitors would help them with their lessons."

One of the sponsored children growing up in the slums of Belo Horizonte in the 1970s was a little girl named Judith. There were ten children in her family, supported primarily by their mother, who, as a seamstress, earned very little. Judith's father was unemployed because of health problems. Like C.U. of India, Judith, at age nine, was on the verge of being taken out of school and sent to work, in her case, as a domestic. Instead, her family was contacted by a CCF worker who was setting up a project in their neighborhood, and Judith became a CCF sponsored child. Today, Judith is an accountant with the huge Brazilian oil company, Petrobras. A large, handsome woman in her early 30s, she majored in American literature at the public university of Minas Gerais.

"Even when I was nine years old," Judith recalls, "I knew that somehow I had to improve my life. But I also knew that without an education this would be impossible." In addition to being able to remain in school, Judith remembers other CCF project benefits, such as health and dental care, hygiene classes, sports activities, and even amateur theatricals. "In the hygiene classes I remember they taught us how to prevent worms," she says with a smile.

Though Judith's economic status has changed dramatically since those days, she still lives in the neighborhood where she grew up. It too, is greatly changed, and she attributes this to the fact that two decades ago, most of the children in the area were sponsored through CCF. "There used to be a little narrow bridge that we called a 'pencil bridge' that stretched over a deep gully," Judith remembers. "The first thing CCF did was to build a strong, stable bridge, and it's still there today. In those days everybody was very poor, but now their conditions have all improved, and it's because of CCF. People have better jobs than they would have had otherwise, and they've been able to help their families. I feel very strongly about what CCF did for us. In fact, I think this kind of aid could resolve the problems of Brazil today."

When the CCF Family Helper project was operating in Judith's neighborhood, it planned to install running water and a sewer, but was unable to do so. Later, however, the former sponsored children and their families managed to get it done, and today the neighborhood has water. Judith is convinced that this occurred because the families, through their association with CCF, were motivated to solve their own problems. Because of the project, she points out, people were organized; they had a place to meet and discuss their needs; and they eventually realized that they could fight to improve their lives. "They fought, and they won," she says

~~~

CCF's transformation beginning during the 1960s from an "adoption" program to an international agency of community development was essential if it was to play a contributing role in contemporary world society. The shift was dramatic, but nonetheless painful for some of those who brought the organization into existence. That Calvitt and Helen Clarke had to leave the organization to permit the transformation to occur left a sour taste in the minds and hearts of those who were close to them. But given the level of the Clarkes' commitment to CCF as an institution and as a world force, no easy transition would have been possible. As for Verent Mills, that other agent of CCF's overseas programs and activities, although he was shifted from pillar to post for a number of years, he remained with CCF. Soon the day would arrive when he would be able to make another indelible imprint on the nature and future of what had become the world's most sophisticated and powerful international agency for the benefit of children.

Chapter Five

FROM CHARITY TO COMMUNITY DEVELOPMENT, 1970-1988

Washington, D.C.—1974

In October of 1974, CCF received an unwelcome, but by most accounts ultimately beneficial shock to its system when the noted journalist Jack Anderson charged in his nationally syndicated column that CCF and other child sponsorship agencies were mishandling donated funds. The charges were triggered by a General Accounting Office study of five major children's charities, commissioned by Senator Walter F. Mondale, Chairman of the Congressional Subcommittee on Children and Youth. While all five charities, including two other child sponsorship organizations, Save the Children and Foster Parents Plan (now PLAN International), were commended for their work in general terms, each was cited for specific instances of poor fiscal management, or misrepresentation of policies to sponsors. Anderson chose to shine his spotlight on CCF, not because the charges against it were the most serious. Rather, of the five agencies under investigation, it was the one with the greatest public recognition.

The lead of Anderson's column was scathing: "The renowned Christian Children's Fund, like the old lady who lived in the shoe, has so many children it doesn't know what to do. Worse, it doesn't know what it did with $25 million, which was raised to feed, clothe, and educate needy children around the world."[1]

Amusing, perhaps, but a significant exaggeration. The published record revealed that one CCF institution in Hong Kong continued to receive sponsorship funds for 118 children for a period of six months after the children were no longer attending the school. When CCF learned of this, the sponsors were assigned other children and CCF ended its association with the school. In Kenya, a project supervisor chose to distribute "designated funds" meant as gifts to specific children among a number of other children who had not received gifts. Several other similar examples pointed to the sloppy handling of funds on the part of affiliate organizations. In CCF's case, the mishandling of only a few thousand dollars was documented—not $25 million.

Testifying before the Mondale Committee, Verent Mills, then executive director of CCF, expressed appreciation to the GAO for bringing these problems to CCF's attention. Indeed, in prepared statements, supplementary documents, financial data, a complete annual audit, and samples of CCF fundraising advertisements, Mills provided more than a hundred pages of documents showing how the organization had investigated each item cited and made across-the-board corrections. And, in rectifying them, CCF instituted new controls for its already tightened financial policies. For example, sponsors were asked to limit the size of special gifts (in 1991 to $20 or less), "unless you indicate the money is for savings, vocational or educational training, a particular need of the child or family, or a special benefit for all the youngsters in the project."[2]

During Mills' presentation to the Committee, Senator Mondale made several telling comments about CCF and the importance of the proceedings. First of all he noted the importance of the manner in which CCF had always raised its money for needy children, "It seems to me that running through this . . . is the apparent fact that one of the best ways to raise money from American donors is on a person-to-person basis. If an American family feels that it can help a child, can become friends through mail, if nothing else, with that child, and give a modest amount on a routine periodic basis, that that is a very powerful attraction for donations. People really like that relationship. It is appealing."

---

[1] Jack Anderson, "The Washington Merry-Go-Round," *Washington Post*, October 1, 1974, p. B15.

[2] "Children's Charities, 1974," Hearings before the Subcommittee on Children and Youth of the Committee on Labor and Public Welfare of the U.S. Senate, October 10, 1974 (Washington: U.S. Government Printing Office, 1974), pp. 1052-1056, 1254-1356, 1387-1401.

He further underscored the point by noting that CCF's donated income in 1967 was $6 million, while by 1973, it had increased to $24 million. CCF, he concluded, "has been one of the most rapidly growing charities in the country."[3]

That October day turned out to be one of the most important days in the history of CCF, comparing favorably with the date Calvitt Clarke dreamed up his "adoption" plan and the date CCF globalized its focus by becoming Christian Children's Fund. From that day forward CCF and some of the other children's charities adopted policies, procedures, and reporting practices that should be able to withstand any level of public scrutiny. From its very first day of existence, CCF depended entirely upon its credibility among donors and the public at large in its efforts to help children. The transformation growing out of the Mondale hearings assured that CCF would forever be very protective of its image and practices.

Among the most immediate changes resulting from the Mondale hearings was a rearrangement of CCF's relationship with affiliated projects, particularly those administered by foreign missionaries. No longer would funds be transmitted to third parties. They would instead be paid directly to the project in the community where assistance was being given.

"There was a drastic change in our policy on 'third party check receivers,'" says Jim Hostetler. "Previously, we had allowed other organizations to deliver sponsorship funds to projects. That practice ended quite abruptly." Within a year or two, all funds were remitted directly to the bank account of each CCF project. This rule is still in force today.

But initially, implementing it took some doing. According to Hostetler, some missionary groups were reluctant to see funds from CCF go directly into the hands of local beneficiaries. In addition, considerable training and preparation of local people were required to ensure that the funds would be properly handled. However, the benefits of the new policy ultimately went beyond fiscal efficiency to the very essence of CCF's work.

"Even before this policy change," says Hostetler, "we began to understand that when outsiders control the purse strings, development is thwarted." Shifting the handling of funds from foreign organizations to local groups and project staff led to the training of local people in recordkeeping, budget preparation and reporting about project activities to the parents of enrolled children. As a result, parents

---

[3] *Ibid.*, pp. 1256-1257.

themselves became involved in financial planning, and eventually in the development of their communities. "Parents could say, 'Why are we paying the teacher so much?' or, 'Why are we spending this much for housing?'"

This type of involvement on the part of parents was a harbinger of things to come—full-scale program planning and operation by the parents of CCF children. Some staff members argued that, logistically, it was easier to transfer funds through international organizations. But when the General Accounting Office found that the Salvation Army in Colombia had been pooling CCF funds for redistribution to several CCF-affiliated Salvation Army institutions, the case for funding local projects directly was compellingly made.

Another important by-product of the Mondale hearings was that CCF along with a number of other child assistance agencies moved quickly to establish a "Code of Fund-Raising Ethics for Voluntary Agencies." Written by development directors representing CCF, Compassion, Foster Parents Plan (now PLAN International), Holt International Children's Services, and Save the Children Federation (most of whom had been involved in the Mondale hearings), the code was formally adopted at a joint meeting held in Chicago on September 8, 1976. Among the principal items of the code were these promises:

- to utilize contributions only as specified by donors
- to maintain the confidentiality of donors
- to use uniform accounting methods
- to minimize overhead costs
- to pay no commissions or finder's fees for new contributors
- to avoid dubious fundraising methods
- to make economical use of fundraising methods
- to be truthful and accurate in all appeals
- to demonstrate respect for people assisted
- to focus always on the welfare of children assisted

The entire code statement was immediately published in CCF's 1975-76 annual report and it has been included in every annual report subsequently.[4]

Not content with a mere general statement of a code of ethics, several of the child assistance agencies further elaborated a fuller code. Adopted by CCF's board of directors on January 23, 1980, CCF's code goes much further in its commitment to "high principles in fund raising." Greater emphasis is placed on truthfulness in appeals, the types of spurious fundraising techniques that will be avoided, and

---

[4] *CCF World News* (Winter 1977), p. 14.

commitments to reduce overhead. But the statement includes two additional specific guarantees: (1) governing directors serve without compensation and may have no financial or other conflict of interest in serving CCF; and (2) CCF is "committed to a policy and practice of full public disclosure of all relevant information concerning agency goals, programs, finances and governance."[5]

The impact of Jack Anderson's revelations on CCF sponsors might have been far less than it was, some feel, had not CCF sent a letter to every sponsor, attempting to reassure them. The result may have been just the opposite. By calling attention to the column, which many sponsors might otherwise have missed, some contributors were almost definitely lost. This was unfortunate since the column painted CCF in a far more unfavorable light than did the actual findings of the Mondale hearings. During CCF's 1975-1976 fiscal year, the first full year following the hearings, CCF's annual income from donations dipped from $28,842,015 to $27,971,370. But the downturn was brief. In the next fiscal year, receipts exceeded $29 million and they have increased every year to the present.

~~~

The Mondale hearings actually fit rather nicely into a program of revitalization and redefinition already well in progress at CCF under the careful hands of Verent Mills. Finally in 1970 upon the retirement of Verbon Kemp, Mills, who had served CCF in almost every other major capacity, became executive director. Although one might have thought that this veteran of 40 years in the service of distressed children—most of those years in association with CCF—could not have any new ideas about CCF's future, Mills began reshaping things almost immediately. And whatever he did must have worked pretty well, since CCF's annual income increased from $17 million in his first year to over $42 million just a decade later.[6]

Mills had always been concerned with the issue of whether CCF's performance matched its image—in short, with the organization's

---

[5] "Code of Minimum Fund-Raising Ethics for Voluntary Agencies in Child Service," *Childworld* (September-October, 1980), p. 22.

[6] Two brief articles summarize many of Mills' achievements: Charles Gregg, "From a Single Orphanage . . . to Global Help for 166,218 Children" and Harlan McMurray, "'Bulldozer Preacher' V. J. Mills: 40 Years of Service to Children," *CCF World News* (Fall 1977), pp. 1, 24. See also Beverly Jacobson, "The Dr. Mills Story," *Childworld* (July-August, September-October and November-December, 1980. January-February and March-April, 1981).

underlying integrity. The more time he spent in Richmond, the more the question gnawed at him: Was CCF actually doing what it told its sponsors it was doing? Though he himself frequently visited institutions and projects around the world, and Dr. and Mrs. Clarke had made their annual global tour as celebrated dignitaries, no one had ever made a scientific study of the impact of CCF's work on the tens of thousands of children it was assisting. In 1972, Mills decided it was time to commission such a study.

"We were saying we were helping these children, and I wanted to know exactly *how* we were helping them," says Mills. "Was it true that we were preparing the children to be better citizens in their communities, as we claimed in our literature? If it wasn't true, then we were wasting the sponsors' money. A financial audit can establish one kind of honesty, but whether you're really doing what you say you're doing and whether the children are reaping the benefit is something else."

To answer this question, Mills in 1972 hired Dr. Charles G. Chakerian, a social scientist from the University of Chicago. Chakerian, who had received his doctorate in sociology from Yale University, had helped establish combined programs in religion and social work at Hartford Theological Center, at McCormick Theological Seminary, and at the University of Chicago. Chakerian was hired to conduct a survey of CCF-assisted orphanages, schools, and Family Helper projects around the world. "Dr. Chakerian spent months personally visiting dozens of our projects," says Mills. "He saw the children and studied their school reports to see how they were doing academically. I called it a program audit, and from 1972 to 1981, during my term as director, they were performed at five-year intervals." Both the CCF Board and the executive staff received copies of the lengthy reports on each institution and project. Weaknesses as well as strengths were fully examined amd reported.

"After Dr. Chakerian completed his audits," Mills continued, "I engaged the services of Dr. Ahti Hailuoto, head of the child welfare department at the International Union for Child Welfare in Geneva, Switzerland, to make a similar audit of the CCF program worldwide. Up until the time I left, CCF was the only agency that had undertaken this type of self-examination."

According to CCF's former director of child and family services David Herrell, the impact of Drs. Chakerian and Hailuoto on CCF's work went far beyond the concept of periodic performance reviews. Herrell, a former student of Dr. Chakerian, says that the sociologist was instrumental in giving CCF a clearer understanding of the needs of children in poverty, and a clearer sense of how the agency should meet those needs.

"Dr. Chakerian helped CCF realize how important it was to critically assess the types of programs being supported," says Herrell. "In the past, such analysis was lacking: to some degree, good intentions on the part of those running specific programs were thought to be enough to ensure that good results would follow."

Chakerian also helped bring several influential child welfare specialists onto CCF's Board of Directors, including Joseph Reid of the Child Welfare League of America, Dr. Kathryn S. Powell, a child development expert, and Dr. Ruth Jewson of the National Council on Family Relations.

"These people prompted a lot of consciousness-raising at CCF about its purpose," says Herrell. "Their message was that you can't effectively help a child apart from the context of his or her family, community, and nation. That context includes the whole pattern of economic and social development. It isn't just a simplistic thing: Help the child."

In addition, Chakerian helped CCF recognize that it would be more effective if it focused on carefully selected countries or areas of countries, rather than, as Herrell puts it, "trying to do a little all over the map. The choice of a location came to depend on whether, by being there, we could influence social and economic development as well as the immediate well-being of the sponsored children."

This new strategy was particularly applicable to Brazil. Since many Brazilian state governments were hostile to social welfare programs, the choice of a field of operations was crucial. As early as 1972, Chakerian traveled with CCF staff members from the Belo Horizonte office to the impoverished Northeastern state of Ceará. In meetings with the mayor of Fortaleza, Ceará's capital, he helped prepare the groundwork for the establishment of CCF's field office in the city and the development there of a multifaceted urban program.

Dr. Hailuoto's analysis of CCF's operations was a factor in the agency's shift from institutions to community-based projects. "He thought we could do more by becoming more community-based," says Herrell. "He argued that by focusing on the education of sponsored children we were really supporting an educational system which drained from, rather than contributed to, local rural development."

Unfortunately, most school curricula in developing countries have been based on academic models left behind by European colonials and are only marginally relevant to the culture and economic conditions prevailing in these countries. "This system took almost anybody who was going to be formally educated 'off the farm,' so to speak," says Herrell. "It prepared many for urban occupations that they couldn't find jobs for, and by doing so it contributed to rapid urbanization and unemployment."

The Finnish sociologist was, in fact, raising a critical issue in development. Mills insists that CCF's aim was never to turn out "little Americans" but to prepare its sponsored children to be better citizens of their own countries. Nevertheless, the effect of most of the education supported by CCF during this period was to Westernize and urbanize the youngsters. It tended to remove them irrevocably from their own, often rural contexts and place them in urban job markets that were frequently unable to support them. Third World cities are full of college graduates driving taxis or working as waiters and chambermaids in five star hotels, while the graduates' home villages stagnate, half-empty, with only old people to work the farms. CCF's earlier tendency to view essentially Western-style education as the greatest gift it could give its sponsored children has now been replaced by a development model concerned with building on the assets and potential of local communities, as exemplified by such ventures as the Family Agricultural School in the Jequintinhonha Valley.

Yet this shift from school-based to community-based projects has not deprived CCF children of access to higher education. On the contrary, both the numbers and proportion of CCF-sponsored children who continue their studies are greater today than ever before, even though the majority will only complete the equivalent of high school, junior high school, or elementary school. As Herrell points out, education cannot be divorced from the general level of development in a particular section of the country. In some remote, undeveloped areas where CCF works today, getting a primary school established can constitute an enormous step forward.

~~~

Hollywood, California—1976

Not only did Verent Mills bring in experts to help redefine CCF's assistance programs, he also engineered a public relations coup just as significant as the movie *Battle Hymn* or the books *Children of Calamity* or *Yankee Si!* during the Clarke years. He brought in a new public relations director in the wake of the Mondale hearings who helped him dream up a new promotional strategy that would make CCF's appeals unforgettable.

Charles Gregg was that development and public relations director. And together they recruited actress Sally Struthers to become CCF's most perennial and utterly effective public voice and image. She was, from the first moment, the most effective spokesperson CCF had ever known. From the time she began promoting CCF in television commercials and in the print media in the fall of 1976, CCF's income increased from $29 million a year to almost $103 million in 1991.

A former fundraiser, publisher and journalist, Gregg brought to CCF a sophistication and flamboyance that proved to be just the right antidote for the agency's sometimes provincial approach to things. Gregg realized that what CCF badly needed was an effective spokesperson. "I got a list of sponsors residing in ZIP codes where celebrities tend to live—Beverly Hills, Park Avenue and the like," Gregg recalls. "Sally's name popped up." She was selected "over greater luminaries," says Gregg, because of the character she was identified with. Gloria Stivic of "All in the Family" was a perfect match for the "typical" CCF sponsor: a young, married, working, middle-class woman.

For someone in a profession that often fosters self-absorption, Sally Struthers is exceptionally outward looking. She grew up in Portland, Oregon, in what she describes as a "lower-middle-income" family that put giving and helping others at the top of their list of priorities. Ms. Struthers remembers the little coin bank in which her grandmother accumulated the money she sent to the Korean orphans she sponsored. Struthers remembers the hand-me-down clothes she grew up in (which in turn were passed on to other children), and the quantities of homegrown peaches her mother would distribute to neighbors in need. Her father, a doctor, was bankrupt when he died. According to Struthers, money meant nothing to him except when he could give it away.

"That's the example I grew up with," she says, "that you always do for others. The joy and pleasure in your life doesn't come from what you do for yourself, but what you do for other people."

When Struthers moved to Los Angeles and became a successful actress, she retained her inbred sense of the importance of giving. And when she landed the part of Gloria in the immensely popular comedy series "All in the Family," success, money and stardom did not change the person she was; in fact, these things only intensified her desire to give. "It was as if I woke up in the middle of the night one night and thought: 'I have to share this.' So I looked around me. My family didn't need help so I had to figure out a way to share what I had, if for no other reason than to spread it around. I just had to start putting it back out there. I saw CCF's ad, and I decided I wanted to sponsor a child."

Struthers had been sponsoring Marites, a little Filipino girl, for a year when she was approached by Gregg about becoming more involved, in a different way, in CCF's activities. Struthers agreed—provisionally—but insisted that she had to have a deeper understanding of CCF's operations. "It's one thing for me to blindly believe you really have all these children and that all these sponsors are really helping them," she told Gregg, "but if you want me to promote CCF, I have to know that the organization is really on the up and up and does what it claims to do."

CCF International chairperson Sally Struthers in Uganda with her soponsored child, Damiano, 1983

Struthers went to Richmond, and spent three days poring through the vast library of files, asking questions and learning how the agency functions. At the end of her visit she was satisfied with what she had seen, but Charles Gregg was not. "We want you to see how it really works in the field," said Gregg. Guatemala was chosen, and after spending more than a week visiting CCF projects there, Struthers was totally convinced. "I'm yours for life," she told Gregg, who was not surprised. He knew that Struthers' grandmother had been a sponsor. In fact, today her mother and her daughter, Samantha, unite four generations of CCF sponsors in a single family.

Verent Mills believes that CCF's extraordinary growth in recent years is due primarily to Sally Struthers and to Charles Gregg's accomplishments as director of development. "Sally has done more for CCF than CCF will ever really realize," he contends. "When Sally came to us in '76, we just took off—she unlocked a gold mine."

CCF doubled, then tripled in size during Sally's first ten years as national chairperson, and during that period advertisements and other promotional activities with which she was associated were responsible for more than 90 percent of the new sponsors who signed up. Struthers is still a major draw for CCF. She is featured in the organization's magazine and television ads. And she continues to generate publicity for CCF through public appearances.

In addition to filming CCF commercials on location at projects around the world, Struthers spends much of her time writing letters and speeches for CCF, accepting awards on behalf of the agency, and giving talks and interviews. In fact, she reluctantly admits, she now spends more time working without pay for CCF than she does acting. But Sally Struthers' commitment to CCF has never wavered. "I think about what all this work has done for the children, and it's a solace for me. Show business is like a troublesome sea—you just float around on it like flotsam—sometimes you're up, sometimes you're down, and it can demolish your self-esteem. One year you have an income and the next year you don't. My work for Christian Children's Fund has been an anchor in that angry sea. Sometimes, motherhood and the work for CCF have been the only things that have kept me going."

Struthers has received countless awards for her work for children over the years. The one she prizes most is the Presidential End Hunger Award given to her in 1990. She has personally sponsored ten children, and she has visited many of them in her travels to film CCF commercials. In particular, she remembers the trip she made to Uganda in 1983, when the country was in the throes of a violent civil war. It was there that she met Damiano, the eight-year-old boy she had been sponsoring for three years.

"The State Department said, 'Don't go. We can't protect you.'" Struthers recalls. She was nervous, but she went anyway. "We landed at Entebbe airport, then nothing but a tin shed riddled with bullet holes. I met Damiano at an abandoned hotel on the edge of Lake Victoria. I had brought a Gucci suitcase full of designer gifts: sneakers, clothes, expensive toys, little trucks, cars, everything. And in the middle of it all I had stuck in a little 49-cent bag of balloons. Well, Damiano had never seen a balloon before. I blew it up for him and his eyes got bigger and bigger. He held that yellow balloon for the next two hours. He didn't care about the toy trucks or the sneakers or the clothes. All he wanted was that yellow balloon. Now he's 15 and he looks wonderful. He's happy, he's healthy and he's doing well in school."

Struthers acknowledges, a bit ruefully, that her involvement with CCF has in some ways begun to eclipse her acting career. "I used to walk down the street and people would call me Gloria, or they'd say 'Where's the Meathead?' (an allusion to her husband on "All in the Family"). Now I'm approached with, 'We really love what you do for the children!'"

Although the work is demanding and the rewards are intangible, she puts great value on promoting CCF. What really matters, she says, is "the end result. I know that thousands upon thousands of children did not go to bed hungry last night because of loving, caring sponsors who are making a difference."[7]

Sally Struthers' effectiveness was examined in a survey conducted in 1989. Though existing CCF sponsors thought her involvement was relatively unimportant to their contributions to the organization, she was identified as second only to Jerry Lewis as a national personality identified with a specific known cause. She ranked far ahead of such other individuals connected with specific charities as Danny Thomas, Art Linkletter, John Ritter, and Sally Field. And among spokespersons for children's organizations she was the only personality respondents could remember.[8] Sally Struthers was another of those virtual godsends that not only saved CCF after the negative Mondale Committee publicity, but enabled the organization to soar to new heights.

~~~

Richmond, Virginia—1980

While Verent Mills continued to build on the foundation of professionalism that had been laid by Verbon Kemp, CCF began to experience a vast expansion in the level of support it could bring to the realm of distressed children around the world. The realigned CCF board of directors, with its experts in such fields as child welfare, social work, nutrition, medicine, administration, banking and finance, now had a truly informed voice in shaping CCF policy. And the revision of financial operations begun in the late 1960s culminated when Mills introduced a fund allocation policy that was for many years the most stringent in the child sponsorship field. Even today, out of every dollar raised, no more than 20 percent is spent on administration and fundraising and 80 percent goes directly into programs.

What, for two decades, set CCF apart from other agencies with similar financial policies was that for CCF, "administration" covered all overseas administrative costs, including those of the international field offices. Other agencies considered these costs to be part of program activities. In 1989, however, CCF adopted a similar approach. Fiscal limitations imposed by the old policy meant that CCF was manage-

---

[7] Natalie Gittelson, "Coming Back Big: Sally Struthers," *McCall's Magazine* (May 1987), pp. 12-13, 16, 20, 23.

[8] From CCF Study Files on Sally Struthers. Struthers' impact on CCF is also detailed in an editorial and article written by Struthers, "Caring, Really and Truly Caring, Takes Courage and Faith and Love," *Childworld* (September-October, 1981), pp. 3-5.

ment starved. In that other organizations in the field counted all overseas expenses as legitimate program expenses, the change in policy seemed appropriate. Of the change, former program director David Herrell says, "It has enabled us to expand the scope of our activities and to do things we couldn't do before."

In 1980, Mills was 67. He had been executive director of CCF for ten years, and had worked with the organization for 34 years. During his time in Richmond (including the many years as second in command to Dr. Clarke and to Verbon Kemp), he had helped to shepherd the agency through the transition from a homespun, family-style operation to a highly respected and efficient international organization. He had circled the globe 14 times during this period — and had had a heart attack while visiting victims of the 1976 earthquake in Guatemala. But with CCF in a strong condition and growing, Mills decided that the time had arrived for his retirement.

When a search committee was appointed to find a new director, 260 candidates applied. The committee's choice was Dr. James MacCracken, Vice President for Program of Save the Children Federation, one of CCF's main "competitors" in the child sponsorship field. MacCracken was also Mills' first choice as successor, although a more different personality from that of the gentle, emotional, rather modest former missionary would be hard to find. MacCracken had a reputation throughout the field as a bright leader and a very hard taskmaster.

Officially installed at a board meeting on July 22, 1981, MacCracken had broad realms of experiences prior to coming to CCF. Born in New York City, MacCracken served in the U.S. Army Air Corps and graduated from Wesleyan University in Middletown, Connecticut. He then taught in Poland from 1946 to 1948 and served with the United Nations International Refugee organization from 1949 until 1952.

He was involved with Church World Service, the overseas relief and humanitarian arm of the National Council of Churches, for a period of 14 years, nine of them as executive director. Next he headed CODEL, a consortium of 34 Protestant and Roman Catholic organizations working internationally in community development. It would have been virtually impossible to find anyone with richer experiences to take on a growing and changing CCF.

MacCracken, when he arrived on the scene at CCF, had nothing but praise for his predecessor, Verent Mills, who saw the organization through its most difficult years and who built its annual budget to the $42 million level. MacCracken also lauded Mills for his work in broadening the racial spectrum of managers in CCF's Richmond headquarters and for promoting a policy of using nationals to run CCF projects and offices. But the difference in the two men's approaches—

and personalities—was immediately evident in MacCracken's management style.

For MacCracken, who joined CCF in July of 1981, an early step in running the organization was to jump-start an unprecedented spurt of growth in the number of children assisted. "I decided to strengthen CCF as much as possible, relying on the existing staff," he recalls with obvious pride. "So I set them a challenge: Could we, in 18 months, grow from 286,000 enrolled children to 325,000?" In fact, the challenge had an ulterior motive. It was the quickest and most

Dr. James McCracken, 4th executive director, with CCF Child in Brazil, 1981

effective way MacCracken knew to discover the strengths and weaknesses of the agency he then headed.

Despite initial doubts and some quiet grumbling among CCF staff, the target date was set for June 30, 1983. By June 17, the number of enrolled children had reached 325,000, and MacCracken declared the campaign a success, ordered a thousand balloons and told the staff to throw a party. When a further plateau of 350,000 was reached some time later, he repeated the celebration. "It was fun!" he says with a touch of mischief.

After increasing the sponsorship base by 14 percent in a year and a half, MacCracken wanted to find out exactly what it was that those 350,000 children were getting from CCF. Over the next three years he visited projects, asked questions and attempted to assess the value of CCF's activities for both children and their communities. MacCracken had impressive qualifications for making such an evaluation. From his years at Save the Children Federation, his work at Church World Service for 14 years, and his experiences with the United Nations, he knew an effective development program when he saw one. He ranked CCF's program "one of the finest I'd ever seen."

From beginning to end, MacCracken quietly focused on CCF's numbers. His annual reports to CCF's board and sponsors bristle with challenges to increase the numbers—of children assisted, of sponsors, and of dollars contributed. Indeed, although CCF had always kept an exact count of the numbers of children assisted, it had not publicized the number of sponsors. MacCracken ensured that each of these figures would always be prominent in the minds of everyone connected with CCF.

In his first report he noted that CCF was assisting 251,000 children. He urged, however, "we can do better!" A year later, he proudly announced that the number had increased to 283,000, but added, "I am confident our growth rate can be even more accelerated, and our services extended to twice—or even thrice—the number of children, their families and communities we are helping at present." The numbers kept soaring as MacCracken and the CCF staff found new and creative ways of expanding the impact of CCF's growing resources. For 1983, he reported 326,993 children assisted. By 1986 the number had grown to 485,734. In his last report as executive director in 1988, he triumphantly announced that the figure had then reached 509,000 or more than twice the number assisted when he arrived seven years earlier.[9]

MacCracken was just as intent when it came to new sponsors and new sponsor dollars. In 1985 he established the practice of counting and reporting each year precisely the number of individuals who were sponsors. In 1985 there were 359,240 compared to 419,094 children being assisted. By 1990 the number of sponsors would increase to the 400,170 level. And to attract more sponsors and more sponsor dollars, MacCracken introduced a sporadic feature titled "Childline: A Quick Read on the Needs of Children." A brief country-by-country report indicated the principal problem for children in each nation and the percentages of populations that were starving, did not have housing or access to potable water, or were uneducated. Unlike photographs of starving and unhealthy children, the Childline report revealed the international scope of the problems CCF was and is trying to address. [10]

During MacCracken's tenure, CCF's annual budget grew to $92 million—twice the level seven years earlier. He is proud of the agency's success in ensuring that the child is the primary beneficiary of CCF programs, even when the programs are community-based. He also took special pride in the fact that in 1987, CCF won a Presidential End Hunger Award from the U.S. Agency for International Development in recognition of its contribution to ending world hunger (three years later Sally Struthers won a similar award for her work with CCF). And,

---

[9] All figures for children assisted taken from CCF annual reports and executive director's reports as published in the fall issues of *Childworld*.

[10] See "Childline" reports, *Childworld* (September-October, 1986), p. 10; (Fall 1988), p. 10.

perhaps surprisingly for a man with a reputation for being tough-minded, MacCracken reveled in the "sense of joy" and the "common vision" that came to permeate CCF during his years there. "That's the thing I feel proudest of," he said upon his retirement in 1988. "If we can't care for each other, how can we care for a child halfway round the world?"

When James MacCracken filed his last executive director's report on October 3, 1988, and therein turned over the reins of office to CCF's fifth executive director in a half century, he did so almost precisely fifty years after the original incorporation of China's Children Fund on October 6, 1938. The transition from MacCracken to Dr. Paul F. McCleary was easy. CCF was financially healthy. Its reputation was secure. Its impact on children around the world was increasing almost geometrically from year to year. It was administratively sound. With a growing number of American sponsors and of international partners around the world, CCF had truly progressed from a simple charity, one among many, to a powerful and responsible development agency. It truly has the power and the resources and the commitment to affect the lives of hundreds of thousands of children, families, and communities around the world.

In its first fifty years CCF had experienced all of the trials and tribulations of a good idea being turned into a good cause, a cause into an organization, and, finally, an organization into a viable, permanent institution. Untold energy and creativity had gone into the founding and development of CCF in the midst of a world torn apart by war. After the cause got going, the major future obstacles had to do with transition from founders to continuing leadership, with a permanent commitment to sound principles, with a constant devotion to effective service to children, and with an unending concern for institutional credibility. Although there had been some fits and starts—the uneasy departure of the Clarkes, too much investment in orphanages and real estate, the Mondale Committee hearings—CCF at age 50 was an extraordinarily healthy and vibrant organization. Its creators, directors, staff, and sponsors had done well and could be justly proud of their institution and its many accomplishments.

However, one thing did not change in the first 50 years of CCF. The needs of children around the world only grew greater. If anything the demand for CCF's programs and services was larger in 1988 than it had been in 1938. The challenges before CCF to find ever more effective ways of delivering its services were abundantly clear. The directions to be taken into the twenty-first century were just in the process of being defined.

SPONSORS

"If it weren't for my daughter's sponsors, we'd be dead."

Richmond, Virginia—1989

Nancy Smith knows little about Third World development, nor is the subject of much interest to her. What she does care very much about, however, is that by sponsoring a child through Christian Children's Fund, she has acquired another daughter.

"I wish I had that first letter with me," said Ms. Smith, who sponsors an 11-year-old girl in Bangalore, India. "It totally charmed me. If I'd had any doubts at all, that letter would have completely eliminated them."

Ms. Smith was attending the opening of an art exhibit at Miller and Rhoads department store in Richmond—the same department store to which Dr. and Mrs. Clarke used to go for quick dinners and iced coffee in the 1950s and early 1960s. On display were paintings and drawings by CCF children from around the world, sent in to CCF, as they are every few years, for exhibition. Ms. Smith was describing how she felt about sponsoring a child, and how moved she was by the first letter she received from the Indian girl, Vasanthi, who was nine years old at the time.

"First of all, she started out by calling me 'Dear Auntie Nancy,'" said Ms. Smith, fairly glowing with affection and pride. "Her letter was very warm and exuberant, which surprised me for such a young child. And she always signs her letters: 'With tight hugs'—which we thought was just wonderful. We've adopted that in our family; now we always give one another 'tight hugs.' My two daughters—they're 24 and 26— they've been writing to her too."

Nancy Smith's attachment to Vasanthi—her eagerness to form and maintain a close relationship with a child halfway around the world—exemplifies the simple human caring that J. Calvitt Clarke believed he could garner for the children of war-torn China when he sent out his first appeal for help in 1938. He was right: Such genuine love on a one-to-one basis has been the lifeblood of the agency for more than 50 years. Ms. Smith, who works for a publisher of educational material, is one of more than 400,000 CCF sponsors around the world. Though the majority of sponsors are Americans, 78,640 of CCF's more than 533,000 enrolled children are assisted with funds raised by CCF's International Partnership Organizations in Germany, Canada, the United Kingdom, Australia, Denmark, Hong Kong, Japan, Korea, New Zealand, France, and Taiwan. In addition, Brazilian sponsors assist 4,186 children in projects in Brazil, and 390 Thai children and 42 Indian children also have sponsors in their own countries. A 1987 demographic survey of CCF's U.S.-based sponsors indicates that 77 percent of these CCF sponsors correspond with their sponsored children. Many also send additional gifts of money, especially for the child's birthday.

As is often the case, details about the specific benefits Vasanthi receives as a result of her sponsor's $21-a-month donation are of little concern to Nancy Smith. She chose CCF primarily because it offered an opportunity for personal contact with a child, although such contact is also offered by several other agencies. And, like most CCF sponsors, she says she was impressed by the fact that "almost all the money actually goes to the welfare of the child." At least 80 percent of CCF funds are used for program activities at the project level; no more than ten percent is spent on administration and fundraising, respectively.

After Smith first contacted CCF and expressed interest in sponsoring a child, she received a photograph of Vasanthi and a folder containing a map of India with basic information about the country under the heading, "Where This Child Lives." Also in the packet was a brief description of Vasanthi's personal characteristics, family circumstances and living conditions, as well as a paragraph describing some of the development activities of CCF projects in India. Such packets are sent to potential sponsors and are updated with yearly progress reports on a sponsored child. A person may agree to sponsor the child in question or not, as he or she chooses. Ms. Smith decided to sponsor Vasanthi, sent in her first monthly contribution of $21, and before long received the child's first letter beginning "Dear Auntie Nancy."

As CCF has grown over the decades from a charitable institution into a development agency, so its use of the sponsorship concept has evolved and expanded. For CCF's Sponsor Services staff today, sponsorship is far more than a mere fundraising tool. "It's our way of educating sponsors about another culture," says Margaret McCullough, Ph.D., who was CCF sponsor services director from 1982 to 1989 before becoming the agency's deputy executive director. "And it helps children understand that there's a 'significant other' who cares about them. I believe the process contributes to better worldwide understanding: I like the idea of connecting family to family. That's what's going to make this world a better place."

While the sponsor communications office in Richmond operates 15 hours a day to respond to the thousands of requests for information that come in by phone and letter every month, national offices and individual projects also have a crucial role to play in maintaining the relationship between sponsor and child. In addition to sending a "welcome letter" to every new sponsor and collecting specific information on each enrolled child's progress in health and personality development as well as performance in school and home activities, many national offices make a special effort to educate sponsors about their country, its culture and traditions, climate and topography, and the particular setting in which the sponsored child lives.

The Ecuador National Office, for example, is one that has shown particular creativity in devising ways to improve and strengthen correspondence with sponsors. "Sponsors and children are both children when it comes to their relationship with each other," says McCullough. "Sponsors should see their child in a holistic sense, in his or her own context." With this goal in mind, project workers in Ecuador ask each child to describe in words or by drawing pictures, "Who I am," "The house I live in," and "My favorite time of year." And on the back of letters to sponsors, the staff list the goals and objectives of the project together with an evaluation of its success in achieving these goals.

Frances McDonald is a retired schoolteacher in Wyoming who sponsors a teenage boy in Kenya. "It's an education I'll never forget—a wonderful education," she says of her correspondence with her sponsored child. "It's a fine geography lesson too. I knew Africa was over there, but from the TV you'd think there's nothing but dust and dirt. When the children write, you really find out something. Their lives are very different from ours. It puts a very human element on what living is all about."

Nevertheless, CCF staff members are sensitive to the need to guard against an approach for which sponsorship agencies have been criticized—that of simply *using* deprived children as a means of raising money. "If an agency lets sponsorship become just a fundraising tool, it degrades the process," says McCullough. "It forces children to 'sing for their supper.' Many agencies put their sponsorship department in with fundraising; we don't. My background was in family social science, not fundraising."

John Schultz, CCF's Sponsor Services Director, sees sponsorship as "a powerful, mind-expanding, consciousness-raising experience for both sponsor and child." Indeed, in addition to correspondence with a child, many sponsors gain increased understanding of Third World conditions, and of the importance of their contributions, through the agency's quarterly publication, *Childworld*, which is free to CCF supporters and other interested persons. The slim magazine (now newspaper format), printed on inexpensive paper, contains articles and photographs depicting the conditions in which children live and the problems they face in developing countries around the world. *Childworld* is intended to inspire a sense of the effectiveness of sponsorship as well as feelings of compassion and concern over the plight of needy children.

Yet many sponsors are learning about the impact of CCF's development approach, both through the materials they receive from the agency, and especially from the letters of their sponsored child. Ruth Matthews sponsors a 12-year-old boy named Marco in a remote rural village in Colombia. In his letters, Marco has described the cooperative farming system introduced by the CCF project to benefit the families of 60 landless peasants, including his father. "The money goes not only to help Marco," explains Ms. Matthews, a contract administrator for a pharmaceutical buying group, who sponsors two other children as well. "It goes to the community through the sponsorship of many children, and some goes to the families to buy farm implements." Marco's letters, says Matthews, are full of information about such crops as chickpeas, wheat and corn, and about the year-round planting season in his area. "One time he wrote describing how green the fields were because of our help. You know, that does something special for you." Matthews has developed an unusual insight into the true scope and sophistication of CCF's activities.

But for many sponsors, what counts most is simply the opportunity to form a close, personal bond with a child. "I enjoy what kids are like inside," says Frances McDonald. "I'm not very good with adults, but I like the direct contact with the kids. I like the idea of writing letters instead of just sending in money. The letters from the kid—for me it's like Christmas all year long."

Ruth Matthews agrees. And though she has never seen Marco, she feels she knows him well. "In one letter that his mother wrote, she said Marco was very shy. Ha!" says Matthews, chuckling indulgently. "He's anything but shy. He writes and scolds me because I don't write often enough. If I don't get a letter back to him right away, I get a reprimand. I've seen changes in him as he gets older. It's great having him around over the years because we can watch him grow up."

Nancy Smith says she feels the same way about Vasanthi. Like many sponsors, she is less concerned about the realities of life in a far-off country than about the joys and sorrows of the little girl she has grown to love. She understands that Vasanthi's schooling, and "some amount of food during the day" are provided by sponsorship funds, but she has never felt the need for more details about project activities. It is Vasanthi's letters — recounting school activities, describing members of her family, or sharing a problem that may be bothering her— that have convinced Smith that she is doing something worthwhile for another human being. "It's like having another child," she says simply. "I can see the growth of this child over the years. It's not only an investment for the child, it's an investment for me as well." When asked how long she plans to continue as a CCF sponsor, Smith looks puzzled, as though the question has never occurred to her. "I've never thought about it," she says. "Probably forever."

While "forever" is a long time, the loyalty of CCF's sponsors over the long term is impressive. Out of more than 400,000 sponsors, 18 percent have been supporting the agency for more than 11 years. Although CCF's policy is to "graduate" a child from sponsorship upon completion of the CCF program, ordinarily at age 18, sponsors are encouraged to begin assisting another child at that time. The survey conducted in 1987 revealed that 78 percent of CCF sponsors said they would be "very likely" to sponsor another child under such circumstances.

It is perhaps paradoxical that the love and concern of sponsors like Nancy Smith, Frances McDonald and Ruth Matthews for individual children is what supports the highly sophisticated, widely varied kinds of development initiatives that CCF implements in the field. In a sense, the agency operates on two levels, relying on personal affection and caring to fund a global network of child welfare, community development, and, ultimately, socioeconomic progress. In fact, this dual approach is highly appropriate, given the agency's roots in the practice of brotherly love and caring for one's neighbor. Indeed, the personal aspect of the sponsorship system finds a parallel in the emphasis on individual human development at the project level. CCF staff members like to point out that although the agency has grown into a leading international child welfare institution, it has never lost sight of the fact that individuals constitute both its fundamental base of support and the ultimate product of its programs.

Moreover, during half a century of using individual contributions for individual human development, CCF has been a pioneer in implementing an approach to solving global problems that is only now beginning to gain wider acceptance. Over the decades, CCF has demonstrated that international child and community development, however vast in scope, simply cannot be effectively achieved through mass, impersonal, bureaucratic measures. It may seem logical—when bombarded by statistics of soaring population growth and the complexity of global problems—to believe that individual, one-to-one efforts are inadequate, mere drops in the ocean of immeasurable human need. But child sponsorship agencies such as CCF—along with a number of grassroots organizations, including those that provide small amounts of credit to microentrepreneurs in Third World countries—are learning that initiatives aimed at individuals are often the only ones that are truly effective. Of course, the logistical challenges involved in serving CCF's 400,000 sponsors and 533,000 children are daunting in their complexity. Nevertheless, more and more development agencies are discovering that such operations can be handled effectively, and that the effort involved is a relatively small price to pay for the tremendous unleashing of human potential that results.

"We had 25,000 outgoing telephone calls and letters to sponsors in the last month alone," says CCF's Sponsor Services Director Schultz, whose division, with 71 full- and part-time employees, is the largest at CCF headquarters in Richmond. Schultz prefers to view each one of those communications as an "opportunity to educate the sponsors about what life is like in other parts of the world. When a sponsor learns that the reason letters take so long in Sierra Leone is that there's no reliable postal system, he or she is being educated."

CCF staff members also emphasize, with pride, the fact that the agency's financial base comes mainly from individuals and recently, to a lesser degree, from corporations, and that the agency has never received any funding from the United States government. As a result of this ironclad policy, CCF has found over the years that it has been able to operate in some countries where relations with the U.S. are poor. CCF is welcome in such places precisely because it is a nongovernmental organization supported entirely by private contributions.

During five decades of using individual donations to care for individual children, CCF has learned what huge bureaucracies like the World Bank or the United Nations Development Programme are only beginning to understand: that the judicious application of small sums with the full particpation of the beneficiaries is the most effective way of relieving economic deprivation. Most CCF sponsors are more generous than they are wealthy. About 30,000 people sponsor more than one child, and a good number of these sponsor up to ten children. One Australian sponsor assists 100 children; a sponsor in Flint, Michigan, 157 children. Then there are the 208 "life sponsors," who have each contributed a one-time amount (currently $4,200 a child). The interest earned by each life sponsorship assists the sponsored child until he or she no longer requires CCF help. At that time, depending upon the sponsor's wishes, the principal may be released to CCF for use where needs are most urgent or used to sponsor another child. Under the latter option, the sponsorship process continues in perpetuity.

Despite the impressive array of "super-sponsors," the majority of CCF sponsors are people of relatively modest means, many of whom make considerable sacrifices in order to sponsor a child. The sponsor relations manager at the CCF national office in Bangalore, India, through which Nancy Smith's Vasanthi is sponsored, asked his projects to conduct an informal survey to determine how many of their sponsors have a second job, or work extra hours, in order to be able to sponsor a child. The 19 projects that participated in the survey reported a total of 83 sponsors in this category: people who hold second jobs as baby-sitters, waiters, dishwashers, house-, office- and hospital-cleaners, salespersons, hairdressers, factory workers, night watchmen, cooks, teachers, office clerks, janitors, horse trainers, housepainters, airplane and automobile mechanics, welders, day care providers, family counselors, farmers, carpenters, dog groomers, park rangers, laundresses, caterers, repairmen and busboys so that they can afford CCF's $21-a-month sponsorship contribution.

In the Winter 1989 issue of *Childworld* there appeared a letter from Marise Meier, a sponsor in Marietta, Georgia:

"When my daughter, Julie Diann, was 12, we decided it would be a nice New Year's project and resolution to help a needy child. We are not wealthy and work extra jobs to pay bills . . .

"When Julie and I went over our budget, I gave her a choice of new (instead of secondhand) clothes, more money for our limited entertainment fund or sponsorship. Her immediate response was, 'Let's sponsor, Mom. We already have all we need.'. . . Thank you for the opportunity to help others and to make us realize how much we really do have."

~~~

Almo, Kentucky—1990

Devin Kerr is a 43-year-old retired Vietnam veteran with three children in college. "I got blown up with a land mine," he explains from his home in Almo, Kentucky, population 250. "I had parts taken out of me and stuff, but I'm doing pretty well."

Mr. Kerr receives Veterans Administration disability payments as well as military retirement benefits, and V.A. funds also help his children with their college tuition. His wife is studying business administration. Over the years, he worked "in different factories." Now he raises peaches, apples, and plums on three and a half acres in a tiny community "that's not even really considered a town," says Kerr. "Only thing we got here is a post office." But a post office is important to Devin Kerr. He drops by there regularly to mail letters to his sponsored child, Tigist, a six-year-old girl living in the slums of Addis Ababa, Ethiopia.

"Our family wasn't poor," Kerr explains when asked about his own background and what it was that made him want to sponsor a child. "Probably the biggest thing that caused me to be like I am was what I saw when I was overseas," he says. "You don't like to see little kids with their bellies all swollen up and no clothes. I saw that in Vietnam and in Korea. When they were really hungry, they'd pick through garbage. American GIs would laugh when the kids fought over C rations or a piece of gum. There are a lot of hungry kids in the world, but most people don't want to know about them. Even my own kids won't look at it on television. It's easier to shut it out than to face it and do something about it."

From the mid-1970s through the mid-1980s, CCF's most effective form of advertising was late-night television commercials featuring the agency's highly popular spokesperson, Sally Struthers, on location visiting CCF projects. CCF's sponsor enrollment grew steadily in 1984 and 1985 when images of the devastating famine in Ethiopia flashed regularly across American television screens.

Devin Kerr signed up to sponsor Tigist in 1987, when Ethiopia was once again threatened by famine, and he happened to see a CCF ad on television. He called the toll-free number given in the ad, although he had no specific country in mind for sponsorship. "I said it didn't matter where, just where the need was the most, and it didn't matter if it was a boy or girl. They came up with Tigist.

"They sent her picture to me on approval," he remembers. "You could either sponsor 'em or turn 'em down. She had those big, sad eyes—that's all it took. It wouldn't have mattered who she was, boy or girl or what color, she just happened to be the one that came to me."

Tigist is a very pretty child: small and delicate, with a sweet face and a beaming, impish smile. She *does* have large, dark eyes, but they are no longer sad. She is a lively, affectionate little girl. As a result of her sponsorship, Tigist's family has been reunited. Tigist's mother, who earns $17 a month cleaning a restaurant, is now able to support her three oldest children, who before were living with relatives, as well as Tigist. When asked who Devin Kerr is, Tigist answers in a quiet little voice, "He's my father."

"A lot of people tried to discourage me from ever doing it," says Kerr.

"They don't believe the money gets to her. And there's prejudice here: I'm white and she's black. Then they say there are a lot of kids in this country who need help too. That's true, but I've always thought that *here* there are ways of getting the help. Besides, I give to charities in this country too."

Early on in his correspondence with Tigist, Kerr discovered he was "hooked." "We wrote back and forth for about a year," he says, "and with each letter I got to care about her a little more." Yet there were aspects of the correspondence that bothered him. In order to communicate with a young child who could neither read nor write English, Kerr had to rely on staff members at Tigist's CCF project to translate his letters into Amharic and the child's letters into English.

Every CCF national office around the world has staff members to coordinate correspondence, including the translation of letters, between sponsors and children. In some cases, individual projects are staffed with at least one person — often a volunteer — who is able to translate letters from English into the local language and vice versa. In other cases, a team of translators at the national office translates all the letters going to and from the country's sponsored children. In a country such as India, which has sixteen major languages, the logistics of translation can be formidable. In the Fortaleza National Office in Northeastern Brazil, in addition to English-Portuguese translators, a team of German-Portuguese translators works on letters to and from children in that area who have German sponsors.

The dusty sponsor relations office at the Addis Ababa National Office is rather Dickensian in looks. There, several earnest-looking translators peck doggedly at elderly manual typewriters translating each and every letter. Although he had received detailed information about Tigist from project personnel, Devin Kerr had many unanswered questions about the child. "After a while you get curious and you really want to see her," he says. "I wanted to see how she really was, was she really being taken care of? I got so I just had to see her." Although only about one percent of sponsors ever visit their CCF child, in March of 1989 Devin Kerr left his home in Kentucky, got on a plane, and flew to Ethiopia to visit Tigist.

"The trip was pretty awful," he says gloomily. "They lost my luggage, so the whole time I was there all I had was one change of clothes." He arrived exhausted and somewhat apprehensive, expecting to find a timid little girl, frightened to meet a strange American. He need not have worried.

"At the airport she came running to meet me," he says with amazement and delight. "She jumped right into my arms with a big bouquet of flowers, kissing me and snuggling me. I had the feeling that she knew me. She ran her hands through my hair because it's so different from theirs, and she was rubbing my face to see if the light color would come off. And she was chattering all the time—I had to keep asking the project people, 'What's she saying?'"

When Kerr visited the slum where Tigist lives, with its flimsy, ramshackle huts and open sewers, he was horrified. He knew that Tigist was receiving various benefits as a result of his sponsorship, but to him these were hardly discernible amid the dirt, dust and crowds jostling for a glimpse of the strange white visitor in the narrow, muddy lane.

"The part that bothered me most was the sewage that ran across her front door," he remembers. "One of the things I noticed is that most every kid there had a runny nose. I think there's a connection with the sewage, the bacteria. Tigist seemed healthy, though, but she's a little skinny." Despite his initial shock, Kerr says he knew the project was doing a good job. "I saw the kids were being fed and they all had clothing, which was more than other kids had. You couldn't tell by their living conditions, but they looked healthier than other kids, and they looked happy. I asked if they'd all had their [immunization] shots and was told that they had. I'm sure what the project is doing is helping. It's just hard to tell when you see how they live for the first time.

"They looked like they were in need of an awful lot of things," says Kerr. "I was really shocked by their school: a little tin building with a dirt floor and no windows—I don't know how they could learn anything. And it was packed with kids, three grades together. The desks were long boards nailed onto posts, and they had another board they were sitting on. They were all sharing books, three or four kids to a book." However inadequate this school seemed to Kerr, he knew that without the CCF project he was helping to support, Tigist and many other children would not have been in school at all. And he is learning that the changes brought about by CCF are a step-by-step process. Since he was in Addis, the agency has replaced the open sewers of Tigist's neighborhood with an underground sewage system.

Visiting Tigist and experiencing the reality of her life had a tremendous impact on Devin Kerr. For a Westerner who has never been to such a place, the actual conditions in which most of the people, including most of the children, live, can hardly be imagined. But regardless of whether they have made journeys such as Kerr's, many well-informed CCF sponsors share his feelings of concern and indignation over the circumstances of a sponsored child's life. A close relationship with a child like Tigist can cause a sponsor to experience, on a deeply personal level, a sense of outrage at the degree of poverty in which the child is growing up, as well as a sense of relief and deep satisfaction that he or she as a sponsor is able to do something about it. This little girl—one of millions living in the slums of African cities—is no longer a faceless statistic to Devin Kerr, but a real child, a child who has become as precious to him as his own, and just as deserving of a decent, happy life.

As is typical when a sponsor visits, the Addis National Office and the project to which Tigist belongs went out of their way to be hospitable and helpful to their guest. "Everybody and his brother knew I was coming," says Kerr. "I was surprised—everybody seemed to know my name. For what they had, they treated me great, like I was something special. I liked every one of them. They were all friendly. Some people wondered why I had come. They thought there must be another reason. You don't come that distance just to see a little girl. The ones who spoke English talked with me a lot. They all seemed real interested and real caring people.

"It scared me at first that I was always surrounded by about 100 people," says Kerr. "They seemed friendly, but you turn around and there's 100 or 200 people all standing there just looking at you. And I thought it was strange that there were donkeys in the street. They said, 'Don't donkeys in America run around in the streets too?'"

Kerr's account of Tigist's visit with her mother to the Addis Ababa Hilton, where he was staying, sounds like a cross between Eloise and Alice in Wonderland. "She had never seen anything like it. When she got into the elevator, she didn't know it was going to move, so she fell on the floor, and when it stopped at my floor she crawled out. When we got into the room, she flipped the electric switches on and off. She went into the bathroom, turned on the water, and then looked under the sink to see where the water went, and she looked behind the television to see where the people were. She'd never been up high before, and she was scared to look out the window. I don't think her mother had seen a whole lot more than Tigist had."

Despite the discomfort and culture shocks, Kerr's visit to Addis was a success, and he hopes to go again. He now corresponds regularly with Tigist's mother, and with project staff as well as with Tigist, and he sends extra money to the project, in addition to his regular sponsorship contribution. "I know they'll use it well," he says. "When I came back I sent some money, and the project put in a water line. Now the community has water right in their area." His commitment to Tigist is such that he has arranged for her to attend a private school, and he hopes that when the time comes she will go to college in the United States.

Like an over-indulgent father, Kerr showers Tigist with gifts, including a giant teddy bear—carried all the way from Kentucky—which is bigger than the child herself. "She was scared of it," says Kerr rather sheepishly. "I guess I overdid it that time. But I still send her anything I can find with teddy bears on it.

"She's like my own kid now," says Kerr. "I've got a fund set up for her college, so she can be something. She has to have the education if she's going to do something that will help people. I won't leave much behind in the world, but maybe this will make a little difference. Anyway, she's worth it."

Few sponsors become as emotionally attached to their sponsored child as Devin Kerr is, but the vast majority do derive a deep sense of satisfaction from the fact that they are making an important, positive difference in the life of a child. And some sponsors have developed creative, and highly cost-effective ways of doing so.

~~~

Falls Church, Virginia—1990

Public Interest Communications is a private telemarketing firm based in Falls Church, Virginia, whose employees are the collective sponsors of four children—in Brazil, the Philippines, Uganda, and Oklahoma.

On May 22, 1990, PIC day supervisor Jim Ress wrote a letter to CCF's Sponsor Communications manager that began this way, "It is with great satisfaction that we are able to enclose this check in the amount of $8,146.50. Currently, forty-five of my fellow employees and I contribute between $1 and $50 each payday to assist our four kids, their families and their communities. And it is with humble pride that we are able to state that our employer matches each contribution dollar for dollar."

The money PIC sent to CCF amounted to much more than the total annual sponsorship contributions of $252 for each of the four sponsored children. An attached sheet requested that the balance be spent on such items as land and livestock, health and diet needs, and education, as well as special birthday and Christmas gifts. While Jim Ress himself donates $50 out of each of his biweekly paychecks to PIC's CCF pool, most of the other employees give about $5 each, biweekly. The total employee contribution amounts to $174 every two weeks, which the company matches.

Some of PIC's money goes to assist a CCF project in the Jequitinhonha Valley in southern Brazil. Gercilia, an unusual person to find in such a remote setting, is in charge of a day care center in a tiny rural community called Funil. Tall, tawny-skinned and attractive with a throaty, husky voice, Gercilia wears her dark hair, fine, clean and shiny, tied in a knot at the top of her head. She also wears round, steel-rimmed "granny" glasses. She has none of the shy, self-effacing characteristics common to poor rural women the world over. Instead, Gercilia is extremely warm, vivacious and outgoing. From the confidence she exudes, one might assume she is a professional: a teacher specializing in early child development, or a social worker employed by the local CCF project.

She works at the project as a teacher, although she attended school only up to the seventh grade. She is employed, not by CCF, but by the local municipality at a salary of $17 a month—less than half the official minimum wage. Gercilia's husband is an unskilled day laborer who is unable, much of the time, to find any work at all. Gercilia has one daughter in her late teens from a previous marriage and a stepdaughter, Andreia.

How does her family survive on so little? "Ah!" says Gercilia, "if it weren't for my daughter's sponsors, we'd be dead."

The sponsors in question—the personnel of PIC—have been assisting Andreia for more than three years. Though Gercilia was able to educate her other daughter only up to the third grade, PIC has already promised to send Andreia to college. Andreia's career choices so far are to be a doctor or a dentist.

"Every three months they send a special gift," says Gercilia, with a touch of wonder in her deep voice. "Several months ago they asked about our home conditions. We had scorpions, bedbugs and *barbeiros* [insects whose bite may transmit the deadly Chagas' disease] living in the walls and roof of our adobe house. We said we needed to do some work on the house, and they sent us the money. Other times they've sent money to buy a sewing machine, a cow, and 13 hectares of land. They write a lot of letters asking what our needs are and then they send the money. The ones who write most are Michael, Jim, Valerie and Julie. On Andreia's birthday they sent a big card and each one wrote a special message. She sends cards for their birthdays too.

"If we hadn't had their help, we'd be in darkness," says Gercilia. "We earn so little here that we could not have built these buildings for the day care center or put in the pipes for our water supply without help from the sponsors of our children."

A substantial proportion of CCF's 400,000 sponsors regularly send extra monetary gifts for the children they assist. Although few do so at the level of PIC, for many sponsored children and their families, these gifts add a small but critically important margin of improvement in the quality of their lives. This is certainly true for Gercilia and her family. And it is true for the family of Sultan, the Ethiopian boy who bought a goat with his special gift. The special gifts are a tangible reflection of the loving bonds that develop between sponsors and children, and which, in a real sense, fuel CCF's entire operation. Yet, it is distressing that, despite CCF's efforts to devise programs that push families beyond mere survival, for some families this goal would not be achieved without special gifts. This is a painful reminder of how deep the needs are. And, given CCF's egalitarian philosophy, it is also notable that in many projects, while some children regularly receive special gifts, other children, who are just as deserving, never do.

Chapter Seven

INTERNATIONAL PARTNERS

The joy of sponsoring a child through Christian Children's Fund is by no means restricted to Americans. True, J. Calvitt Clarke established the agency in 1938 because he believed that his relatively affluent countrymen had a responsibility to come to the aid of children in need, even during a depression, and even if the children happened to be on the other side of the world. Today, however, the agency Clarke founded truly encompasses the globe. Some 79,000 sponsors in 12 countries other than the United States are providing assistance to needy children, either through the CCF international office in Richmond or through programs administered in 12 other countries on the CCF model. These International Partnership Organizations (IPOs) account for 20 percent of all CCF sponsorships; together with CCF in Richmond, they form the World Alliance of Christian Children's Funds. Clearly, when Clarke decided to appeal to Americans to help children in China, he could not know all that he was starting.

Canada, 1960

As might be expected, Canadians were the first "international partners" to sign on. When CCF started advertising in magazines after World War II, many Canadian readers (who represent between five and 10 percent of the audience for U.S. publications) responded. It was only natural that ties between CCF and Canada should be especially strong: Verent Mills himself is Canadian, as were a number of the missionaries in Asia who ran CCF-assisted orphanages in the early years. CCF's first cottage plan orphanage in Japan, the Bott Memorial

Home, which, though no longer affiliated with CCF, still exists as a children's home, was named for Dr. Ernest Bott, the first professional social welfare worker sent to Japan by the United Church of Canada.

As the Canadian sponsorship base grew, it eventually became necessary to establish Christian Children's Fund of Canada to provide tax deductions for Canadian sponsors. As part of Dr. Clarke's prolific correspondence with sponsors, he had begun in the late 1950s to receive complaints from Canadian sponsors that their contributions to the U.S.-based Christian Children's Fund were not deductible from Canadian income taxes. Soon, Verent Mills (on one of many trips from his base in Hong Kong) was dispatched to London, Ontario, to investigate the possibility of establishing an official, Canadian branch of CCF. Through the Rev. James Duncan, a Presbyterian minister who had been superintendent of one of CCF's orphanages in Kalimpong, India, Mills was put in contact with the Rev. Watkin Roberts of Toronto.

Rev. Roberts' past experience as a missionary in Asia was unusual, to say the least. In 1910, he had felt called upon to send a copy of the Gospel According to St. John to an isolated tribe of headhunters in the district of Manipur in northeastern India. He later spent a number of years living with the tribe, and converted them to a nondenominational Christianity which they practice to this day. The tribe eventually turned from hunting heads to preaching Christianity among neighboring communities in Burma and Bangladesh, as well as in the Indian state of Assam. The church Roberts helped establish in Manipur remains unaffiliated with any other, and has always been run exclusively by members of the tribe itself, never by outsiders.

Together with Frank Whilsmith, an advertising executive who later served as chairman of its board and national director, Roberts laid the groundwork for the establishment of Christian Children's Fund of Canada. The new CCF affiliate opened an office in Toronto in 1960 (presently the office is in Scarborough, near Toronto). From then on, Canadian support became an important part of CCF's activities in Korea, Japan, Taiwan, and Hong Kong. Indeed, the buildings that house the CCF offices in both Taiwan and Bangalore, India, were purchased with Canadian funds. But as time went on, CCF-Canada, wanting to make more than a financial contribution to the agency's activities, became interested in administering projects directly.

Their interest was well timed. By the early 1970s, CCF was operating in more than 50 countries, and the board of directors felt that some of its projects were so remote from the nearest national office that adequate monitoring was difficult. In the efforts to improve the fiscal oversight of field operations, the Richmond board decided to ask CCF-Canada to take over the administration of a number of institutional projects in Sri Lanka, Jamaica, Barbados, and Nicaragua.

Today, 13,500 of Canada's 29,000 sponsorships are channeled to CCF-Canada's own programs in 14 countries. Some are in countries—such as Burkina Faso—where CCF has never operated. And although CCF-Canada's development approach is very similar to that of CCF, two policy differences prevail. All of CCF-Canada's projects are church-affiliated, though they too serve children of many faiths. And while CCF has always staunchly declined U.S. government support, CCF-Canada receives about 20 percent of its funding from the Canadian government. This is because, says CCF-Canada's national director Peter Harris, "there are no strings attached," an assertion that is substantiated by more than a quarter century of experience.

With characteristic Canadian generosity, CCF-Canada donated more than $500,000 (Canadian) of Canadian government funds as a special grant to CCF's Antigua national office for disaster relief after Hurricane Hugo in 1989. CCF-Canada has also made arrangements to assist orphaned and abandoned children in two countries that have been devastated by brutal dictatorships, Cambodia and Romania. And, in partnership with CCF, CCF-Canada has launched a fundraising campaign to ensure that the children of Hong Kong who need care will be provided for, both before and after the absorption of Hong Kong by the People's Republic of China in 1997.

In 1990, Christian Children's Fund of Canada received a letter of commendation from Canadian Prime Minister Brian Mulroney, which declared, in part, "The Christian Children's Fund of Canada, in providing assistance overseas, is contributing to the promotion of self-sufficiency among all the nations of the world, and in so doing, is securing our future and that of our children. Through the compassion and generosity of its membership, the Christian Children's Fund of Canada is doing much to enhance the notion of the world as a warm and caring place."

~~~

Denmark, 1972

The establishment of CCF's second international partnership organization—in Denmark in 1972—was the unplanned effect of the power of journalistic persuasion.

In the late 1960s, Morten Pedersen was editor-in-chief of *B.T.*, the largest daily newspaper in Denmark. On one of his many trips to the United States, Pedersen learned of CCF and became so fascinated with its work that he began to assign reporters from his newspaper to travel to Africa and write articles about CCF projects. At first, his secretary fielded the flood of calls from readers demanding to know how they could sponsor a child. She helped them send money to Richmond as best she could. But when the eager Danish sponsors-to-be became too numerous to handle, her boss—and the CCF board in Richmond—decided it was time to open a Danish branch of CCF. In 1972, Pedersen became national director of CCF-BOERNEfonden, Danish for Children's Fund.

It is not surprising that Scandinavians should be major supporters of CCF. Of the world's rich, industrialized countries, the three that spend the largest portions of their gross national product on aid to developing nations are Norway (1.17 percent), Denmark (0.93 percent) and Sweden (0.90 percent). The United States, though the second largest donor in monetary terms (after Japan), ranks number 18 in the list in terms of percentage of GNP, spending 0.21 percent, a smaller portion than does Ireland. Today, BOERNEfonden assists 27,000 children. Approximately 2,400 of its sponsors are in Sweden, Norway, and Finland. Some 7,200 of BOERNEfonden's sponsored children are assisted through the Richmond office, while the remainder are served by independent BOERNEfonden projects in two tiny, densely populated, environmentally fragile African nations: Rwanda and Cape Verde. In Rwanda, BOERNEfonden's annual budget is larger than that of the national Ministry of Social Welfare. The current national director is Soeren Stenum.

~~~

Japan, 1974

In 1974, CCF's international partnership organization in Japan became the first to "graduate" from recipient to donor status. In doing so, it set a pattern which has been followed by a number of other CCF organizations in former beneficiary nations. CCF hopes that this transformation will eventually be a natural step in all the countries where the agency is active today.

By 1968—20 years after CCF first began sponsoring children in war-ravaged Japan—it was becoming increasingly clear that in Japan's booming economy, support from a foreign charitable institution was less and less necessary. Indeed, the Japanese government was already assuming increasing financial responsibility for CCF's orphanages, to the point where, by the early '70s, CCF's support represented only two to three percent of the total operating costs of the Japanese institutions. CCF decided, therefore, that it would withdraw entirely from Japan by 1974.

In 1971, in recognition of CCF's role in salvaging and rehabilitating more than 80,000 Japanese children after World War II, Verent Mills was invited by Crown Prince Akihito and Princess Michiko to the Imperial Palace for the presentation of a medallion of appreciation on behalf of the Japanese people. It so happened that on the morning of the presentation, Princess Michiko had been watching a television interview with Mills. When the interviewer expressed gratitude for the work of CCF over the years, Mills replied, "Don't thank me. Your gratitude should go to the American and Canadian sponsors of Japanese children over the years."

When it was time for the award ceremony that afternoon, Princess Michiko was prepared. "Please express our thanks to your American and Canadian sponsors," she said.

But Mills did better than that. The staff and the board of directors of CCF in Japan had already begun to examine how best to express their thanks to the agency and its sponsors, and also how they could best continue CCF's work in the future. In discussions with David Otani, CCF's national director in Japan and a professor of social work at Izumi College, which CCF had founded in 1960, Mills said: "There's no need to return your thanks to us. Instead, why don't you show your thanks by giving your assistance to needy children in your neighboring countries? There must be some generous Japanese citizens willing to become sponsors, just like our American and Canadian sponsors."

There were. By the time CCF finished its work in Japan in 1974, there were 13 Japanese sponsors, all of them Rotarians who had learned of CCF through the Rotary Club magazine, and who were prepared to support the fledgling Japanese organization with considerably more than the monthly sponsorship amount of 4,000 yen (at that time about $15). In addition, Mr. Otani had taken a number of heads of CCF institutions on an exploratory Asian tour to determine which countries most needed assistance. These individuals also agreed to become sponsors of the new Japanese agency, which was named Christian Child Welfare Association of Japan, or CCWA (pronounced Sisi-Wa).

CCWA's choice of Korea and the Philippines as countries to assist is highly significant, because it reflects the attitude of many present-day Japanese toward their country's bellicose behavior during the earlier decades of this century. Takeshi Kobayashi, who succeeded Otani as National Director of CCWA, puts it this way: "CCWA is in Korea and the Philippines because we Japanese are very conscious of what we did in the war." With a mixture of proper Japanese reserve and boyish openness, the dynamic young director explains that today, many of CCWA's most active sponsors are former soldiers in the Japanese army. It was their bittersweet memories of the Philippines from the perspective of an occupying army that prompted many of them to sponsor Filipino children through CCWA.

When David Otani, CCWA's first national director, applied for routine government clearance to begin assisting the first 67 Filipino children in 1975, he discovered that CCWA was embarking on uncharted waters. Japan's social welfare regulations did not cover the export of charitable funds overseas, a process for which there was no precedent. But Otani, who had been with CCF since the mid-1960s, was undeterred.

"We explained to the officials," he said in his careful, heavily accented English, "'Look, we Japanese have been assisted by a foreign organization called CCF for the past 26 years, for such a big number of children and by such a big amount of American dollars. Now Japan has become quite prosperous. Why do we not do the same thing to other so-called developing countries?' They said, 'If you want to do so, you go ahead. But we cannot give you official permission.' So we had to get special permission from the Bank of Japan and from the Ministry of Finance."

Today, CCWA assists over 5,000 children in community-based projects in the Philippines. Though its approach is modeled after CCF's, CCWA has gone one step further in terms of endowing beneficiaries with decision-making powers. The force behind this move has been young Kobayashi himself. Kobayashi had spent nearly ten years in the Philippines, both as a student of social work and later as a field worker for CCWA. He had observed that sponsorship tended to divide communities between sponsored and non-sponsored children, and to create jealousy on the part of families whose children were not sponsored. His solution was to set up parents' committees in a project area before children were assigned for sponsorship, and to ask the parents themselves to assess the needs of the families in their community and decide which children should be sponsored.

In accordance with CCF tradition, CCWA does not accept Japanese government funds. The reason directly addresses the issue of large-scale, high-cost development as opposed to CCF's—and CCWA's—small-scale, community-based approach. "CCWA is trying to achieve development at the community level," says Kobayashi. "We are not for the development on a big scale. If we received such big money [from the government] we might have to force our projects to consume these financial resources in a way that was not in the people's best interests. I don't like the situation where only the people from the developed country take the initiative. I'd like to develop this organization hand in hand with our partners in the developing countries. Also, it is very important to get support from Japanese ordinary people. Relying on private money forces us to maintain a high quality relationship between sponsors and children. If we had government money it would be much more difficult to evaluate our work."

In 1989, Japan became the world's most generous donor of assistance to developing countries in monetary terms, with an expenditure of $8.96 billion. In terms of foreign aid as a percentage of GNP, however, Japan ranks 12th among industrialized countries, after, among others, Australia, Italy, and Germany. David Otani believes that CCWA's emphasis on child sponsorship can be a means of educating the Japanese public about the humanitarian potential of their country's economic might in an increasingly interdependent world.

"The Japanese people have been awakening to their responsibility to developing countries, as citizens of transnational or borderless communities," he says. "Japanese people are not accustomed to think about the people outside Japan, so our effort to educate our people is being accelerated year by year. It might take much longer than we expect, but it has begun."

~~~

Hong Kong, 1977

Although each of CCF's International Partnership Organizations is unique, having come into being as a result of particular needs or capacities of its own country, the experience of Hong Kong is perhaps the most distinct of them all. For one thing, it is the only International Partnership Organization in which sponsorship no longer plays any part.

From the time mainland China fell to the Communists in 1949 until a decade later when Verent Mills was recalled from Hong Kong to Richmond, the Hong Kong office of Christian Children's Fund was the headquarters for all of the agency's international field operations. The administration of CCF-assisted institutions throughout Asia, the Middle East and Europe, as well as the processing of all the sponsored children's files—including case histories, photographs and progress reports—was coordinated through the Hong Kong office. This was regardless of whether the child lived in Taiwan or Finland, in Japan, Lebanon, or Italy. In addition, Hong Kong itself—a haven for millions of Chinese refugees—was the site of some of CCF's finest orphanages, notably the beautiful Children's Garden, as well as the Clarke Children's Home and the Pine Hill Babies Home.

When CCF's overseas operations center moved with Mills to Richmond, the Hong Kong office was still occupied in administering CCF's Hong Kong orphanages and the various "rooftop schools" the agency had created on the tops of high-rise tenement buildings. But during the 1960s and early 1970s, the CCF orphanages were gradually transferred to local control and support, until, by 1977, CCF's role had been phased out completely. Pine Hill is now a home for handicapped children, run by The Hong Kong Mentally Handicapped Association. Children's Garden, now called Wu Kwai Sa Youth Village, was donated to the Hong Kong YMCA for its youth programs—some of which, in fact, served the children who attended the rooftop schools in the teeming H-block buildings where they lived.

As the government of Hong Kong began building schools and day care centers in the increasingly prosperous colony, rooftop schools were no longer needed. CCF then shifted its attention to the children's social and psychological needs, and to the family and behavioral problems that are often created by rapid industrialization and urbanization. Among other things, the agency founded a school of social work to train counselors and caseworkers to help deal with these emerging needs.

By the time CCF left Hong Kong in 1977, the school was almost wholly supported by the local government. Furthermore, the name of the former CCF office had been changed to The Hongkong Children & Youth Services. Today, this agency assists several group homes for children from dysfunctional families. It also serves children with special needs who have been referred by the school system, the courts, or the police, and administers after-school programs for "latchkey" children.

Despite its autonomy, The Hongkong Children & Youth Services has not been entirely cut loose from the CCF system. Concern for the future of deprived children in Hong Kong, especially in light of the uncertainties posed by the pending takeover of the British colony by the People's Republic of China in 1997, has prompted both CCF and CCF-Canada to launch a fundraising campaign called Children's Trust 1997. Already there is evidence of dwindling local support, and increased demand, for the kind of child welfare programs provided by Hongkong Children & Youth Services and other such agencies. By appealing to the ethnic Chinese communities in North America, Christian Children's Fund is working to ensure that in the potentially turbulent years ahead, the welfare of the children of Hong Kong will not be forgotten. That is the greatest challenge facing Mary-L. Beyns, current director of the agency.

~~~

Germany, 1978

CCF Kinderhilfswerk, Germany's CCF partnership organization, was founded in 1978 by Karin Astrid Greiner, a very energetic CCF sponsor. She was born in the Netherlands where she spent her early childhood years and where she made her first acquaintance with a black person. This was an American GI who, right at the end of the Second World War, handed her a piece of chocolate. "It was the first time I ate chocolate," she remembered later, "and I thought that only colored people could give such wonderful things. So I decided to love these wonderful people of color."

At age 11 she moved to São Paulo, Brazil, with her parents. There she passed a slum every day on her way to school. Feeling sorry for the impoverished children in the area, she began sharing her lunch with one or two of them. When she told her mother of her modest philanthropies, her mother said that it makes no sense to give something to someone just from time to time. "You have to help people continuously to make a difference," the mother Greiner proclaimed.

As a young woman Astrid Greiner moved to the United States and there became a CCF sponsor. When she later returned to Germany with her husband and two small children, she immediately set about persuading her friends and acquaintances to sponsor Brazilian children through CCF. Shortly, 45 of them agreed to do so. When in 1978 Verent Mills was looking for someone in Germany to build up a German partnership organization, he located Astrid. With little urging, she agreed to set up an office in her hometown of Nuertingen, south of Stuttgart, and she became the first national director of the affiliate.

There was some logic in this appointment. After the Second World War, thousands of German children had been helped by CCF. More than $6 million had been sent to assist German orphans. When Germany made its spectacular economic recovery and the standard of living in Germany increased to one of the highest in the world, it was only appropriate that Germans should return the favor through CCF. Many remembered the time during the war when they almost starved from the lack of food, when housing was destroyed, when they did not have the clothes to stay warm or the fuel to heat their homes. When prosperity returned, many Germans felt responsible to help out elsewhere in the world. As a result there are in 1992 approximately 20,000 charity organizations in Germany. Although the nation and its people are tangling with a host of economic difficulties resulting from reunification, millions still contribute to charities.

"In the early 1980s as the economy grew and grew, we received so many letters each day that we often needed laundry baskets to get them into the office," a member of the Kinderhilfswerk staff remembers. During the 13 years Astrid Greiner was national director, about 40,000 Germans became sponsors. Today almost 20,000 Germans sponsor a CCF child in a developing country. Due to Astrid's special interests, 9,000 of them assist children in Brazil: 7,000 through the Fortaleza national office in the northeast and 2,000 through the Belo Horizonte office in the middle of the vast nation. In 1990 she took a trip to visit some of the projects in South America. Her rediscovery of the people and the continent was so powerful that in 1991 she moved to Lima, Peru.

Mrs. Greiner's successor at Kinderhilfswerk is Conny Wolf, a committed young economics and marketing specialist. Over a three-year association with the organization she has built up the marketing and advertising program. In addition to directing the 14-person staff, she also coordinates all of Kinderhilfswerk's advertising. The current chairman of the board is Dr. Karl-Ernst Huedepohl, who lived and worked in both Africa and South America for many years. He, too, knows the problems of the Third World very well.

~~~

Great Britain, 1983

The idea for an international fundraising network made up of affiliates of Christian Children's Fund originated in the early 1980s with Charles Gregg, CCF's Director of Development from 1975 to 1991. Gregg was raised in Brussels, and with his decidedly international perspective, he was convinced that CCF's sponsorship approach would appeal to a wide range of donors throughout the world, and that, especially among the populations of English-speaking countries, a vast reserve of potential support was waiting to be tapped.

According to Robert J. H. Edwards, a chartered accountant who is the national director of Christian Children's Fund of Great Britain, Great Britain is indeed fertile ground for attracting CCF sponsors. Nevertheless, the challenges are formidable and the competition is stiff. There is no question that the English are philanthropically inclined: When CCF first opened an office in London in 1983, it joined some 350,000 British charities—all of them "dedicated to separating people from their money." Today, CCF-Great Britain ranks among the 100 largest charities in Britain, an impressive accomplishment, considering that there were nine other child sponsorship agencies on the scene before CCF arrived, all of them addressing their needs to the British donor market.

In this setting, the print and Christmas card advertising campaign of CCF-Great Britain has been highly effective, and its growth has been remarkable. During its first year, 2,500 sponsors signed up, and by 1990 the number of children with British sponsors had reached 16,204. While CCF contributed to the British office's operating costs for its first four years, by the fifth year, the office had become financially self-sufficient.

No quaint English mustiness clings to CCF-Great Britain. It has developed a lively and sophisticated approach to attracting sponsors. A television advertising campaign has been carefully planned and a strategy devised to induce British corporations to support specific project activities, such as the building of a school or the installation of a well. Even the handling of British sponsorship funds is high-tech. Only 20 percent of British sponsors make their contributions through the mail, and those who do receive a yearly voucher rather than the monthly receipts sent to U.S. sponsors. The vast majority of British sponsors use "direct banking," whereby their monthly donations are automatically deducted from their bank accounts.

~~~

Australia, 1985

Friendships dating from World War II laid the groundwork for the creation of a Christian Children's Fund of Australia. After Christian Children's Fund of Great Britain was well and truly launched, Dr. Thomas Murrell, then President of CCF's board in Richmond, began to survey his contacts for the right person to set up an Australian fundraising organization. During his wartime service in the medical corps, Murrell, a noted dermatologist, had encountered an Australian colleague, Dr. Adrian Johnson. In 1984, Murrell visited Johnson in Australia and convinced him to put together a board of directors for an Australian CCF. Johnson's first two recruits were a nationally known attorney and the former governor of the state of New South Wales, Sir Roden Cutler.

"There was a special bond between Dr. Johnson and Sir Roden," says Robert Brooks, CCF-Australia's national director. "During the War, Sir Roden Cutler had distinguished himself at the battle of Damour River in Lebanon by capturing three enemy machine-gun posts single-handedly. He was later awarded the Victoria Cross, the British Commonwealth's highest award for valor. But in the course of that action, Sir Roden received a leg injury which ultimately resulted in the amputation of his leg. He lay wounded on a hillside at the battlefield for 27 hours, until Dr. Johnson, his friend from university days, went out with two stretcher-bearers—at considerable risk—searching for him. They finally found Sir Roden, nigh unto death, and brought him back. And it was Johnson himself who, for some days, nursed Sir Roden until his condition stabilized. Sir Roden owed his life to Dr. Johnson."

When Johnson asked Cutler to serve as Chairman of the Board of CCF-Australia, Cutler was glad to accommodate his old friend. Cutler's popularity as governor of New South Wales, his prominence, and his connections as a businessman and former chairman of the State Bank of New South Wales got the new CCF affiliate off to just the right start. Such connections have been invaluable to CCF-Australia, since CCF was by no means the first such agency to introduce child sponsorship to the Australian public. World Vision has dominated the field there for the past 30 years, according to Brooks, and Foster Parents Plan (now PLAN International) is also well established. The rapid growth of Christian Children's Fund of Australia to 12,100 sponsored children in its first six years was therefore all the more impressive.

CCF-Australia first began advertising in July 1985. Brooks was appointed national director in October 1985. Following Dr. Johnson's death, William Joris was elected chairman in December 1988.

~~~

Taiwan, 1985

It is perhaps ironic that, more than 50 years after CCF was founded to assist children in China, one of the agency's greatest success stories should be the other China, the Republic of China, 120 miles from the mainland on the island of Taiwan.

CCF first established an orphanage in Taiwan in 1950, when the impoverished island was absorbing floods of refugees from the Communist mainland. In 1964, a CCF national office was opened in the city of Taichung to administer family helper projects on the island. By 1970, 24,000 Taiwanese children were being sponsored.

In 1974, CCF's social science consultant, Dr. Charles Chakerian, visited the Taiwan office as part of his worldwide survey of CCF projects. After studying the economic and social conditions on the island, he recommended that the Taiwan operation begin to prepare for independence. This was not because Taiwanese children no longer needed the assistance and services sponsorship could provide, but because the young island nation had become prosperous enough for local sponsors to begin to support the program themselves. Charles Tung-Yau Kuo, an enthusiastic Taiwanese social worker who had been superintendent of a family helper project since 1964, was appointed national director in 1976, and one year later, a plan was drawn up to begin advertising for local sponsors.

CCF offered to help pay the advertising costs, but the confident and imaginative Kuo preferred a more direct, "in-house" approach. He asked his staff to "tell the story" of CCF to their relatives and ask for donations, offering a prize to the employee who brought in the largest contribution. Not surprisingly, perhaps, the winner turned out to be Kuo himself. Next, he asked all project superintendents to invite wealthy members from the surrounding communities to form advisory committees to help with fundraising. The target set for the first year was 300 local sponsors and $3 million New Taiwan (NT) dollars; Kuo signed on 328 sponsors and raised $5 million NT.

The second year, he asked each staff member to write "a nice story about a sponsor coming to visit a child, or about our children who are now grown up and want to give something back—a success story." They were to submit their stories to local newspapers and magazines, and Kuo promised to match the amounts the publications paid if the stories were bought. This tactic worked so well that before long, news reporters were hounding the CCF office for more "nice stories." "So we stopped rewarding our staff for their writing," says Kuo simply. By 1981, at the end of four years, Christian Children's Fund of Taiwan had 8,000 local sponsors—more, in fact, than they could handle—and they had spent no money on advertising.

When, in 1985, CCF phased out of field operations on Taiwan, the newly independent agency changed its name to Chinese Children's Fund. Today, its budget is larger than that of all the other child welfare agencies operating on the island—Taiwanese and foreign—combined. "Our sponsor increase is faster than our needy children's increase," says Kuo triumphantly. "Every week about 100 new sponsors contact us, but we tell them we already have around 1,000 people waiting to sponsor a child."

In 1987, the Chinese Children's Fund of Taiwan did what no former CCF beneficiary organization has done before or since. It began providing sponsors for CCF in Richmond, to assist CCF children in different parts of the world. Today, 4,800 CCF sponsors are Taiwanese. Since Kuo has more potential donors than needy Taiwanese children, he tries to induce prospective sponsors to sign up for a child through CCF: the U.S. monthly sponsorship contribution is only $21, while it costs $40 to sponsor a Taiwanese child. And whereas children are always immediately available for sponsorship through CCF, there is a four- to five-month waiting list for those who choose to sponsor a Taiwanese child. Nevertheless, most Taiwanese sponsors prefer to wait and contribute more.

With frequent sponsor-to-child and child-to-sponsor visits, picnics, garden parties, summer camp, winter camp, community chests and an "alumni association" of former sponsored children who counsel and encourage project beneficiaries, Chinese Children's Fund programs obviously generate a great deal of goodwill and community solidarity. And they provide some services the parent agency never dreamed of—such as "homemakers" who care for children when their mothers are away, or training for women who wish to set up day care centers in their homes. Most imaginative of all, perhaps, are the group therapy sessions for widows, part of a program called "Second Spring." "If the widows want to remarry," says Kuo in his eager, near-perfect English, "we announce in the newspaper that we have several widows who prefer to remarry, if some men would like to make friends with them. Then we arrange for them to meet and have a picnic."

Although widows are enjoying their "second spring," the fact is that there is less and less need for the monthly contributions and caseworker visits that have characterized Taiwan's family helper projects. The Taiwanese standard of living has risen so rapidly in recent years that in one day at an unskilled job, a mother can earn more than half of the standard monthly contribution amount. But although the needs are no longer strictly economic, Kuo has begun to grapple with new and more sinister threats to the welfare of children: child abuse and neglect, and dysfunctional families.

"Just one year ago, nobody [would] believe Taiwan has some child abuse cases," says Kuo, "so we make calculation from newspapers. After six months we find about 800 cases—that means each month about 120 cases, every day four cases. We published that in the newspaper, and now government know this and they are concerned about it. So government asked CCF to arrange foster care, and money was provided from the government." Through a process of caseworker interviews, careful screening and negotiations with parents, the agency has placed some 300 children in temporary or long-term foster homes, either to protect them from abuse or to ensure that they receive the care their parents are unable to provide. Counseling for parents is also part of the program.

~~~

Korea, 1986

"As the old national organizations have been turned loose," says Jim Hostetler, formerly CCF's regional coordinator for Asia, "each has developed approaches that are quite different from those employed by CCF." The Korean CCF organization is a case in point.

When Korea Children's Foundation was officially established in 1986, its director, distinguished public health physician Youn Keun Cha, had already spent ten years as CCF's national director. During that time he set out, in a sense, to undo the work CCF had done in the preceding decades, by reuniting institutionalized children with their families.

Large numbers of Korean children had needed institutional care during the 1950s, 1960s and early 1970s, in part because economic and social pressures often drove families to give up a child born out of wedlock. Either the disgrace was too much to bear, or the mother's financial situation did not allow her to raise the child. "They would be abandoned as infants," says Hostetler, who spent 14 years with CCF in Korea, "laid on the doorstep of a small neighborhood police station. People were confident that the child would be looked after. If there were pressures in the family, the escape route was that the child could be institutionalized."

But CCF had come to realize that institutionalizing children who had families was really not the best thing for the children. In the late 1970s, Dr. Cha learned—through newspaper accounts and his own inquiries—that many families had had a change of heart over the years and were in fact searching for their abandoned children in the labyrinth of Korea's institutional system. "There might be a single mother who never stopped remembering that she had a child, and the time comes when her circumstances allow her to reclaim that child," says Hostetler. "People do change their minds about giving up children. It might have been a decision made by one member of the family, and later other members wish they could find the child."

On May 1, 1986, at the request of the Korean Ministry of Health and Social Affairs, the Korea Children's Foundation opened its Child Find Center. The government pays all the program's expenses, and has arranged for access to all official records on child placement. KCF also has very extensive placement files. The government provided KCF with a telephone number to encourage relatives of missing children to come forward. Soon after opening, the Center began to advertise in newspapers, and on millions of government-manufactured cigarette packs, seeking to locate children who had been lost since infancy. As of April 1992, the Child Find Center had reunited 1,241 children with their families.

Although the program has been a huge success, it is actually only a sideline for KCF. In preparation for its independence in 1986 from CCF, KCF had launched in 1977 a campaign to attract local sponsors. By 1991 KCF's 60,000 Korean sponsors were assisting 22,800 Korean children in 19 Community Welfare Centers (similar to family helper projects) throughout the country, and 26,800 children in 358 institutions. Many of the latter were orphans, and others were handicapped children unclaimed by their families. Despite the success of the Child

Find campaign, Cha laments the fact that institutional care continues to be needed. "If we could reduce the number of children abandoned by their parents," he says, "then our child welfare program for needy children would decrease abruptly. But in Korea, a big problem in the child welfare field is that the parents—mostly unwed mothers—still abandon the children." KCF has established a program designed to encourage mothers to keep their children. It offers family counseling, financial support, and job training.

More and more, KCF is also turning its attention to the social ills that threaten the welfare of many children in Korea. In 1987, KCF conducted a survey in collaboration with UNICEF to find out why large numbers of children continue to be abandoned. In 1988, KCF served in an advisory capacity to the Korean government as it revised its Charter for Children. That same year, KCF organized the first symposium on child abuse and neglect ever held in Korea, and, in 1989, the agency was instrumental in founding a National Committee on the Prevention of Child Abuse and Neglect. In the future, KCF intends to focus on assistance to children suffering from behavioral problems. It is also planning to go international. In 1990, Cha toured a number of African countries in preparation for launching a campaign to encourage Koreans to sponsor African children through KCF.

The new programs being developed by KCF, Chinese Children's Fund, and The Hongkong Children & Youth Services have evolved spontaneously as a response to the needs of children in increasingly wealthy, developing industrialized nations. These programs, such as the provision of foster care, or counseling for abusive parents, suggest some of the directions child welfare agencies naturally take as their focus on the care of children shifts from survival and development to broad social concerns.

It was the special vulnerability of children to the devastation of war that impelled Calvitt Clarke to found CCF in the 1930s; it was the vulnerability of children to economic deprivation that impelled the agency to shift its focus toward development in the 1960s; and it was the vulnerability of children to family breakdown and alienation resulting from rapid economic growth and urbanization that has prompted CCF's new International Partnership Organizations to meet the needs of children in affluent societies today. Whether the need is for shelter and food, for education and economic opportunity or for family counseling and foster care, Clarke's "supply of needy youngsters" remains abundant. Perhaps it always will.

~~~

New Zealand, 1990

In 1987 and 1988 Robert Brooks, the national director of CCF in Australia, investigated the possibility of establishing a branch in New Zealand. On each occasion he found it impractical due to the fact that New Zealand had only one television network. TV New Zealand was owned by the government, had limited advertising, and charged enormous prices for the little it did carry. The possibility of affordable advertising costs was remote.

When a commercial television station commenced in 1989, the situation changed. As Brooks looked at the new situation, it appeared that a start was possible. Charles Gregg of CCF went with Brooks to New Zealand and determined that a commercial advertising campaign might be successful.

An experiment was undertaken resulting in 800 inquiries during the first week and 344 contributing sponsors. Brooks and his associates worked until 9 p.m. every night to handle the deluge of inquiries. An office was soon opened, later to be located at 200 Victoria Street in Auckland.

Part of the initial success was due to the involvement of well-known athlete and television producer Allison Roe, who became a sponsor and appeared in CCF advertising. This gave CCF instant credibility and continuity since she also joined the initial board of directors. After twenty months there were 6,120 paying sponsorships in a country with a population of only 3.5 million. The only CCF country with a higher per capita rate of sponsorship is Denmark.

The board of directors for CCF-New Zealand was established in January 1990 with William Joris as chairman along with various members from CCF-Australia. Jill Eagle was named office manager.

~~~

France, 1990

Until 1989, no American or British sponsorship agencies—in fact, only CARE among all child care organizations—had ever attempted fundraising in France. This was largely due to a false perception that the French are too nationalistic and self-centered for such a program to succeed.

In September 1989, however, CCF's Executive Director Dr. Paul F. McCleary decided to stop over in Paris on his way back to Richmond, after attending an international CCF conference in Hamburg exploring possibilities for programs in Eastern Europe. With him was CCF development director Charles Gregg, who grew up in Belgium and who speaks French fluently.

Once in Paris, the two invited the handful of CCF's French sponsors residing in the Paris area to a small reception. Out of 41, 29 attended! From this nucleus began the "naissance" of CCF-France—which took the name of one of France's most popular songs of the past two decades: Jacques Duteil's "Prenez un Enfant par la Main" (Take a Child by the Hand). The French agency was officially authorized and welcomed as a CCF international partnership organization in April 1990. The charter chairman of the French Board of Directors is Jean-Pierre Cabouat, former French ambassador to Canada, French Consul General in Washington, D.C., and chairman of the 1989 French Bicentennial celebration.

~~~

The story of the World Alliance of Christian Children's Funds is far from over—in fact, in terms of its potential growth, it has just begun. Five countries currently assisted by CCF—Brazil, Thailand, India, Guatemala and Mexico—have started local sponsorship programs of their own. These are countries with a substantial middle class, where the pool of potential sponsors is significant. Though the process is slow, self-sufficiency remains the goal, for CCF national offices in recipient countries as well as for individual CCF beneficiaries.

Chapter Eight

"RIGHTS OF THE CHILD": A NEW ERA

Christian Children's Fund, now a venerable half-century old, secure in its past, and seeking to respond to the challenges of the future, has been joined by quite a few others in declaring that we must all be concerned about the world's children. The way in which they have joined is quite notable—through the enactment of international laws and treaties. And through the adoption of an internationally accepted declaration of just what are the rights of the world's children. All of this action has fundamentally altered the status of children in the world, has established a legal framework in which the actions of nations and leaders of governments may be measured, and has promised new generations of children that they have legal standing.

The process culminated, interestingly, on the bicentennial of the development of the two most significant statements of human rights in world history. It was in 1789 that the United States Congress drafted and sent to the states twelve amendments to the U.S. Constitution, ten of which were ratified and would be forever known as the United States Bill of Rights, setting forth fundamental rights reserved to every American. At the same time in France, the National Assembly drafted and issued the famous Declaration of the Rights of Man and of the Citizen, distilling into one document those legal and political rights that would be guaranteed to all French citizens and that should be established for all peoples everywhere. These two declarations have been probably the most important documents that set forth and still protect basic human rights for people throughout the world.

A declaration on the rights of children, properly written and suitably adopted, should over the next centuries have the same moral

Girls in a CCF project in Guatemala benefit from the project school, clinic and nutritious meals.

and legal force. The process began in 1979 during the International Year of the Child. At that time the United States and 42 other nations began drafting a Convention on the Rights of the Child. This was to be a treaty document that would address the economic, social, religious, cultural, civil, and political rights of all children. It particularly was to define the obligations of governments and of adults toward children. Although the Convention had been drafted and considerable consensus reached among the various nations representing many cultures and ideological differences, it lay dormant until 1989 when the Polish delegation to the United Nations moved that the Convention be placed before the UN General Assembly. It was approved unanimously by the General Assembly in November 1989, subject to ratification by 20 signatory nations. On September 4, 1990, with the necessary number of approvals, the Convention went into effect with the force of law. Christian Children's Fund took a strong position in favor of the adoption of the Convention and in promoting the first phases of implementation.

Just a few short weeks following ratification, 71 heads of government convened in New York to participate in the first World Summit for Children. The Summit gathered on September 30, 1990, and with

President George Bush of the United States among those present, adopted a Declaration and Plan of Action to follow the dictates of the Convention.

Since this epochal document on the rights of children has set the stage for CCF's work in the coming years, it is important to pause long enough to grasp the scope of the Convention. In summary, these major rights were enunciated:

- The child's right to life: a society's obligation to ensure the survival and maximum development of its children.
  The right to a name from birth, and to citizenship of the country of birth if the child benefits from no other.
- The right that the child's best interests prevail in all legal and administrative decisions, taking into account his or her opinions.
- The right to protection from discrimination.
- The right to live with parents unless this is deemed incompatible with the child's best interests; the right to maintain contact with both parents; society's obligation to provide information when separation results from society's action.
- The right to leave or enter any country and to maintain regular contact for family reunification.
- The right to be protected from kidnapping or retention abroad by a parent or third party.
- The right to express an opinion and to have that opinion heard.
- The right to seek, receive and impart information through the media of choice.
- The right of freedom of thought, conscience and religion.
- The right to protection of privacy.
- The right that the child's parents or guardians be regarded by law and society as those with the primary responsibility for their children.
- The right to protection from all forms of maltreatment by parents or others, and to preventive and treatment programs in this regard.
- The right to receive special protection and assistance from society when the child is deprived of family environment and to be provided with alternative family care or institutional placement.
- The right to have the process of adoption regulated.
- The right of refugee children, or those seeking refugee status, to be assured of special protection and the cooperation of competent organizations providing such protection and assistance.
- The right of handicapped children to special care and training designed to help achieve self-reliance and a full and active life in society.

- The right to the highest standard of health and access to medical services; society's obligation to ensure primary and preventive health care, health care for expectant mothers, health education, the reduction of infant and child mortality and the abolition of harmful traditional practices.
- The right of children placed by the state for reasons of care, protection or treatment to have all aspects of that placement evaluated regularly.
- The right to benefit from social security.
- The right to an adequate standard of living: society's obligation to assist parents who cannot meet this responsibility and to try to recover maintenance for the child from persons having financial responsibility, both within the state and from abroad.
- The right to education; society's obligation to provide free and compulsory primary education, to ensure equal access to secondary and higher education and to ensure that school discipline reflects the child's human dignity.
- The right to an education directed toward developing the child's personality and talents, preparing the child for active life as an adult, fostering respect for basic human rights and developing respect for the child's own cultural and national values and those of others.
- The right of children of minority communities and indigenous populations to enjoy their own culture and to practice their own religion and language.
- The right to leisure, play and participation in cultural and artistic activities.
- The right to be protected from economic exploitation and from engaging in work that constitutes a threat to health, education, and development; the right to have minimum ages set for employment and to have conditions of employment regulated.
- The right to protection from illegal narcotic and psychotropic drugs and from involvement in their production or distribution.
- The right to protection from sexual exploitation and abuse, including prostitution and involvement in pornography.
- The right not to be sold, trafficked or abducted.
- The right of child victims of abuse, neglect, exploitation or torture to physical and psychological recovery and social reintegration.
- The right of accused children to be treated with dignity, without arbitrary detention, torture, cruel and inhuman treatment or punishment, life imprisonment and capital punishment; the right to be presumed innocent until proven guilty in prompt and fair trial; the right to legal or other assistance; the right to be detained separately from adults, to maintain contact with family, and to

129

receive a sentence based on rehabilitation rather than punishment.
- The right not to have to take a direct part in hostilities, that no child under 18 be recruited into the armed forces, and that all children affected by armed conflict benefit from protection and care.[1]

While CCF was still promoting the adoption of the declaration of rights for children, it described the potential effects of such a Convention as "an important instrument in a global strategy for the protection of children." Legislators could use it in each country "to make children a higher priority." For agencies such as CCF it would become "the moral code by which we can demand the protection of children." True to this pledge, CCF has made this statement the cornerstone of its ambitious plans for the 21st century.

Just as important in the immediate range are the goals of the Plan of Action adopted by the World Summit for Children. Seven overarching goals were established to be achieved through the concert of nations and private sector organizations such as CCF by the year 2000. Briefly described they are these:

1. Reduction of the 1990 under-five child mortality rates by one third or to a level of 70 per 1,000 live births, whichever is the greater reduction. This goal could be achieved by attacking the causes of 60% of these deaths, i.e., diarrheal disease, measles, tetanus, whooping cough, and pneumonia.

2. Reduction of maternal mortality rates to half of the 1990 levels. This goal could be reached by making available elementary, low-cost prenatal care.

3. Reduction of severe and moderate malnutrition among under-five children by one half of the 1990 levels. This goal could be reached, at an annual cost of only $10 per child, principally through educational programs on child care, feeding, and the prevention of common illnesses.

4. Universal access to safe drinking water and to sanitary means of excreta disposal. This goal could be achieved with an average initial investment of $30 a person and annual recurring costs of under $2 a person.

5. Universal access to basic education and completion of primary education by at least 80% of primary school age children. This goal could be achieved by using low-cost strategies to provide a minimum of five years of basic education in even the poorest nations.

---

[1] "Standing Up for Children's Rights," *Childworld* (Autumn 1989), pp. 18-19.

Children in Zambia enjoy a meal provided through the services of a CCF project.

6. Reduction of the adult illiteracy rate to at least half of the 1990 level, with emphasis on female literacy. This goal will require attention to women, who constitute two thirds of the 900 million adults in the world who cannot read or write.

7. Protection of children in especially difficult circumstances, particularly in situations of armed conflict. This goal requires attention to 80 million children exploited in the workplace and 30 million who live on streets.[2]

The goals are, by and large, practical in their direction and capable of achievement through concerted action. Moreover, they provide clear guidance for CCF and other development organizations to choose their own objectives and means of participation.

What is most important, however, is that through the auspices of the United Nations, there is for the first time in human history an agreed upon protocol and procedure for addressing the needs of the world's children.

---

[2] This version of the seven goals is abstracted from a document prepared by Paul F. McCleary, "Keeping the Promise: Ten Steps to 2000" (typescript, December 26, 1990), pp. 2-4.

Chapter Nine

CCF'S GLOBAL PLAN OF ACTION

While the United Nations Convention on the Rights of the Child was duly ratified in September 1990, and while over the next year more than a hundred nations signed the declaration, Christian Children's Fund wasted not a moment in defining how it would respond to the challenges and oppportunities of the new era. Indeed, it would seem from an early vantage point that destiny, challenge, and opportunities for CCF converged by 1990 so that the sixth decade of its existence will be a time of even greater involvement in the welfare of children in all corners of the world. The immediate indications are that CCF, under the leadership and guidance of a devoted board of directors and an energetic executive director, has seized the moment to fill a great international void just as did J. Calvitt Clarke and a tiny band of Richmond folk in 1938 when war displaced the children of China.

Dr. Paul F. McCleary came to Christian Children's Fund in 1988 upon the retirement of Dr. James MacCracken. Like MacCracken he arrived by way of Save the Children Federation where he served briefly as acting president and Chief Executive Officer. But for 30 years prior to that he held a variety of capacities in the United Methodist Church and with the National Council of Churches. For 12 of those years he was a missionary in Bolivia. For another host of years he oversaw international ministries for the United Methodist Church and for the National Council of Churches. He was well prepared to take on the administration of CCF and to guide its rendezvous with destiny.[1]

As soon as he came to CCF he began outlining the challenges of the

---

[1] Don Murray, "Introducing Paul McCleary," *Childworld* (Fall 1988), p. 20.

1990s and the 21st century. In his first annual report he described "The World of the Child of the 1990s" and called for the adoption of the United Nations Convention on the Rights of the Child. Whereas CCF had so frequently talked about starving, homeless, and displaced children, McCleary became a prophet and outlined the consequences of earthshaking changes occurring in the Soviet Union, Germany, Iraq, Poland, and South Africa. Trends in population growth, economies and debt in the Third World, and environmental degradation were outlined

Dr. Paul F. McCleary 5th CCF executive director, 1986-present

in crisp and cogent detail. The world's 5 billionth child was born about that time and McCleary described what his or her life must be like since 93% of the world's population lives in virtual poverty.[2]

McCleary had been fully sensitized to real poverty during his 12 years in Bolivia. The hardest thing about being the pastor of a parish in rural Bolivia in the late 1950s and early 1960s, he says, was burying the children. "When the icy southern winds came up and hit the Andean range, children used to fall ill with respiratory diseases. Since they were already severely malnourished, there could be 15 to 20 children in one small community who died every year. And you knew that the medical profession was incapable of doing anything about it. Doctors were writing prescriptions, but the people couldn't fill them because they had no money."

Bolivia has long been the second poorest country in the Western Hemisphere, surpassed only by Haiti in its infant mortality rate, malnutrition, illiteracy, and pitifully low standard of living. Those years he and his wife, Rachel, spent in Bolivia were at once painful, frustrating, rewarding and highly instructive; what he learned there proved to be the ideal preparation for his current role at CCF.

---

[2] Paul F. McCleary, "The World of the Child of the 1990s," *Childworld* (Autumn 1989), pp. 4-7.

The Methodist pastor's sense of compassion grew strong from his firsthand experience in Bolivia. "It got so I could tell when parents would begin to develop a psychological distance from every newborn child," says McCleary. "Since they were never sure whether or not the child would live, they didn't want to get too attached." The profound, inescapable conclusion that McCleary reached in his windswept, dirt-poor parish is one that countless churchmen and women have adopted in reconciling their deepest religious convictions with the daily horrors they witness in their work. "How can the church be the church only on Sundays?" asks McCleary. "Either it's irrelevant, or it struggles to transform the daily life of the congregation." Indeed, this eminently practical and necessary impulse of Christianity has been the underlying motive-power of CCF's work since its beginnings in war-torn China.

Paul McCleary and Verent Mills have been the only CCF executive directors who had hands-on experience working in developing countries before assuming the leadership of the organization. "My wife and I were in Bolivia long enough to see, firsthand, all the manifestations of poverty and the terrible impact it has on people," says McCleary. "Working among the poorest, we were exposed to the full spectrum of problems that poverty breeds—high infant mortality, annual pregnancies, malnutrition, low productivity, low income, as well as the repetition of the poverty cycle from one generation to the next. As a pastor, again and again you witnessed the poverty cycle reappearing—you saw the children growing up in the same circumstances as their parents. So for me, it's not at all difficult to know what people must be experiencing in Brazil or India or the Philippines, and to have a strong, empathetic relationship with the staff who are attempting to change things.

"Macroeconomic development is not really development," says McCleary. "Unless the family itself is involved, all you're doing is reinforcing the existing political and social structures. That's why the one-to-one sponsorship idea [of CCF], rather than large, one-shot injections of money, is a much more realistic way of achieving true development."

Given McCleary's background in the field as well as his involvement in designing and directing global efforts, it was perhaps logical that he would take the challenge of the United Nations' Convention on the Rights of the Child and the World Summit's Declaration and Plan of Action in 1990 to devise a global plan of action for Christian Children's Fund. In less than three months following the World Summit, McCleary and the organization's program planners had articulated CCF's own statement of goals, "Ten Steps to 2000." The document represents one of the clearest statements ever issued by CCF setting forth in rather precise terms its global plans.

The "Ten Steps" are not only responsive to the UN Convention and

Carolyn Watson

These children in a CCF project in Kenya have found that developing a friendship through letters is one of the most rewarding aspects of sponsorship for both child and sponsor.

the World Summit. They also grow out of CCF's recently revised and focused mission statement:

> Under the Judeo-Christian ethic of helping our neighbor without regard to race, creed, nationality or sex, Christian Children's Fund and its international associated organizations are dedicated to serving the needs of children worldwide—primarily through person-to-person programs, in the context of the family and community, and using a developmental approach through national and local partners.

Implementation of this mission meant that CCF would need to develop, maintain, and/or expand programs in three broad realms, including:
- Child survival, or helping to save and conserve life.
- Child development, or helping provide a quality to life.
- Child protection, or helping protect the rights of children.

While these aims and concepts were not new to CCF, they came to be sharply focused as CCF participated in the World Summit and joined in various implementing conferences looking specifically at health issues or education.

The Ten Steps, then, constitute a set of promises CCF pledges to keep in each of these realms to sponsors, children, and parents of CCF's children:

CHILD SURVIVAL

1. We pledge that every child enrolled in a CCF project will be immunized against the basic childhood diseases (measles, whooping cough, tetanus, diphtheria, mumps, poliomyelitis) and, where appropriate and necessary, immunized against other diseases and protected against malaria;

2. We pledge that every child enrolled in a CCF project will have access to primary health care and to dental health care;

CHILD DEVELOPMENT

3. We pledge that every child enrolled in a CCF project will be provided the nutritional conditions for him/herself and appropriate instruction for the family so that malnutrition will be eradicated;

4. We pledge that every child enrolled in a CCF project will have access to safe drinking water;

5. We pledge that every child enrolled in a CCF project will have access to basic education—every child above age eight will be able to read and write; and, to the degree possible, the child's parents will be taught as well;

6. We pledge that every child enrolled in a CCF project will be taught the means to alleviate poverty and its consequences through income generation projects and/or vocational training appropriate to the situation;

CHILD PROTECTION

7. We pledge that we will affirm child protection and support the role of the family as the primary care giver and protector of the child in order that every child may know what it means to belong to others whether these be the natural parents or adoptive ones;

8. We pledge that we will support environmentally appropriate development to conserve the world's natural resources for the present and future generations of children;

9. We pledge that we will protect the rights of the child as they apply to survival and development, parental care, labor, education, religion and expecially as they pertain to one's own dignity as a member of the human race;

10. We pledge that we will assist every child within our means who is found in especially difficult circumstances—such as orphans, street children, refugee or displaced children, children of socially disadvan-

Dr. McCleary visits with a CCF assisted child in Thailand. 1992

taged families, those exposed to the perils of war, natural disaster, or radiation and chemicals—to be free from extraordinary risks constraining their normal development.[3]

The "Ten Steps" not only cover the seven technical goals articulated by the World Summit, but also set forth CCF's strong commitment to affirming the crucial role of the family, to protecting the environment, and to alleviating the causes of poverty.

But even as CCF and McCleary were developing this broad agenda for the 1990s, some important new tools were being put into place to make it possible to carry out this global plan. ChildAlert is one of the most important of these, innovative in concept, yet reminiscent of CCF in its earliest days. ChildAlert, created in January 1990, and operated separately from CCF's traditional sponsorship program, enables CCF to intervene in crisis spots or to respond to special needs of specific groups of children at high risk.

The program allows CCF, according to McCleary, to assist some of

---

[3]Mission statement and "Ten Steps" are abstracted from Paul F. McCleary, "Keeping the Promise: Ten Steps to 2000" (typescript, December 26, 1990), pp. 4-6, and as revised in October 1991. Also, Memorandum, Paul F. McCleary to Don Murray, September 14, 1991.

those millions of children around the globe who are not only needy, but who live in especially difficult circumstances. "CCF must constantly respond to—must 'take its agenda from'—the ever-changing environment and circumstances in which the world's children live," he says.

These include street children, children with one parent, children who survived natural disasters such as earthquakes, droughts, typhoons and epidemics, children who are refugees and victims of war, and children affected by AIDS. ChildAlert is sustained by a special, non-sponsorship fund to which CCF supporters and other donors are encouraged to contribute. ChildAlert extends year-long grants, renewable for up to three years, to indigenous agencies throughout the world which have programs designed to meet the emergency needs of especially vulnerable children.

"Through ChildAlert, we have the capacity to respond to the needs of any child anywhere in the world," says McCleary with a note of triumph in his voice. "Sponsorship is a long-term involvement that builds development, but it's also somewhat inflexible in that it ties our resources to a specific child in a specific place. As the world changes, new needs emerge and sponsorship is not always capable of reaching the most needy child as quickly as is necessary. Of course we will continue to meet the long-term needs of children in the context of their families and communities. But at the same time we'll have a compassionate concern for any child who has an unusual need. That's what ChildAlert is all about."

In accordance with this objective, ChildAlert in its first two years of existence has committed $1,648,274 through 52 grants. These include an anti-cholera strategy in Latin American countries where CCF works, an AIDS prevention program in Uganda, assistance to a South African rehabilitative center for children traumatized by violence, and emergency relief to Kurdish refugees in the Persian Gulf War.

"We seek out these organizations through our national offices and other networks," says McCleary. "We're particularly concerned about certain regions—the Middle East, Africa, Central America—where war and civil strife are having a devastating impact on women and children. In a sense, the front page dictates where we turn our attention."

A 1990 listing of ChildAlert grants reflects the broad diversity of problems the program can tackle:

- Malaysia: $40,000 to provide counseling for Vietnamese boat children subjected to violence by pirates
- Ethiopia: $30,000 in food grants for children caught in famine and civil war
- Namibia: $44,000 for victims of the recent war for independence
- Hong Kong: $30,800 to care for unaccompanied Vietnamese

refugee children held in detention centers
- Philippines: $174,200 to assist earthquake victims
- India: $50,000 to help cyclone victims build more storm resistant homes
- U.S.A: $68,000 to provide health and social services for Richmond at-risk children in a slum neighborhood[4]

Emergency relief for children victimized by war and devastation is where CCF began. After more than half a century, it has come full circle. Since its founding in 1938 for the specific purpose of assisting Chinese children displaced and orphaned by war, CCF has expanded and transformed itself into a leading practitioner of the most sophisticated, innovative and effective approach to child-centered development known. Yet for McCleary, this evolution would not be complete if it did not, once again, also embrace children who need more immediate and more specialized assistance. Today, the lessons learned over the decades enable CCF to make informed decisions in selecting emergency programs to be assisted. "We want to focus ChildAlert in a way that it leads to [family and community] development," says McCleary, "so that it's a prelude to development."

Concomitant with ChildAlert are two additional initiatives designed to enable CCF to intervene in crisis areas not associated with the poverty and ills of the Third World. ChildEurope and ChildChina programs recognize the need for CCF to serve children everywhere in the world. Both were launched in early 1990: ChildEurope to enable CCF to intevene in Europe where chaotic changes in government and disasters such as the Chernobyl nuclear plant meltdown were putting thousands upon thousands of children at risk; ChildChina to enable individuals to assure the future of needy children in Hong Kong when that crown colony is returned to China in 1997. Although these initiatives could perhaps be seen as impinging upon CCF's longstanding concentration on the Third World, they are essential in the organization's movement toward globalization.[5]

CCF also plans to call upon the expertise of its international staff by assigning national directors and other executives to undertake special activities. Hence, Rolando Torres, a physician who is national director of the Guatemala CCF office, now serves a three-year stint as CCF's roving public health consultant. "We want him to survey all our areas of operation to determine what kind of public health programs we

---

[4] For a full listing of 1990 ChildAlert grants, see *Childworld* (Autumn 1990), pp. 6, 10.

[5] See especially Paul McCleary's annual report in *Childworld* (Autumn 1990), pp. 6-7, and his report "Restoring CCF's Momentum for Human Development," Appendix I, Executive Director's Report to Board of Directors (July 1990).

should be supporting around the world, what specific health services we should be providing in the different regions, and which health networks we should be working with," says McCleary.

The special tragedy of institutionalized children in Romania triggered a major new CCF initiative. With all types of family planning banned under the Ceausescu regime (toppled in late 1989), thousands of unwanted children were abandoned to bleak, impoverished, state-run orphanages. There the often-brutal, always neglectful treatment they received frequently resulted in profound physical and emotional impairment. To determine how CCF could best assist these children, Carol Mickelsen, then the agency's finance director, was sent to open an office in Bucharest. "We see our task as assisting children who should not be institutionalized by moving them away from an institutional environment to as near a family setting as we can. Sponsorship is a logical vehicle, but we don't know how viable it is or what accommodations we will need to make," says McCleary. Recalling the experience of Korea Children's Foundation in reuniting institutionalized children with their families, McCleary hopes CCF can provide similar services to Romanian families.

CCF's new initiatives and its hundreds of existing projects around the globe are impressive, benefiting, as they do, well over a million people. Yet when one considers the vast, seemingly endless numbers of children and families in need, one cannot escape the gnawing doubt that all such efforts, despite their magnitude, are merely a drop in the ocean of want. Paul McCleary's response is simple: "It's the constantly falling drops of water that consistently wear away the stone," he says.

"The month-to-month value of a single sponsorship is very modest. But over time—and it can take 15 or 20 years—the human value of this assistance as a rule far exceeds its cumulative financial value. It's the consistency and the perseverance, rather than the quantity, that bring lasting results.

"People learn most rapidly by example, by seeing and imitating," says McCleary. "When you have a community where significant change is taking place because of health care or irrigation or fresh water or proper sewage management, neighboring villages see the difference and they imitate what they see, even when we don't have a project in their community. The issue is not that we have to respond directly to everybody's need. If we set up village-level, grass-roots programs that can be replicated, others can see their value. People see that the children are happier and healthier and they want to replicate that." As just one example of this process, CCF can cite a request for assistance in reducing the high incidence of hepatitis B in Indonesia. CCF arranged for all the children in its Indonesian projects to be inoculated. Within six months, the government had done the same thing throughout the entire country.

CCF has been evolving into a truly global organization over the past decade. But because of new innovations and shifts of emphasis in the past few years, the process is accelerating. CCF's Richmond headquarters, in McCleary's words, "is being removed from center-stage." Changing relationships with former CCF beneficiary nations and with fundraising partners have spawned the World Alliance of Christian Children's Funds. On November 1, 1990, during that very eventful six-month period that saw the international transformation of the status of children, CCF and nine of its international partners came together to create a novel World Alliance to assure coordination between and among Christian Children's Funds in Australia, Canada, Denmark, Germany, Great Britain, Hong Kong, Japan, Korea, Taiwan, and the U.S.A. After two years of discussion, the ten organizations came together "to provide an international network of organizations the ability to respond more effectively and efficiently to the needs of children around the world." The Alliance was conceived as not only a coordinating body, but also a leader in "advocacy for the protection of children."[6]

In many ways the Alliance is becoming as important to CCF's overall perspective and operation as the Richmond-based headquarters. "There is a myopia that can afflict development agencies," says McCleary. "They tend to regard developing countries from the perspective of the United States. But when you look at Asia, you see that the countries that today exert the greatest influence on development are Japan and the 'Four Little Dragons'—Korea, Taiwan, Hong Kong and Singapore. In the future, their economic and development policies will have far more influence on Indonesia and the Philippines than will ours. By formalizing and strengthening our relations with these countries, CCF is approaching the world holistically. We recognize that we can't do it all alone. Our strength is in our partnerships—our Asian partners and our European partners. CCF now has the capacity to make decisions through the Alliance that will be much more appropriate to the problems and cultures of the countries they affect."

Another important step in CCF's globalization has been the establishment of liaison offices in New York and Geneva. These are the cities where the United Nations and its subsidiary organizations, various church groups and the International Committee of the Red Cross are

---

[6] "The World Alliance of Christian Children's Funds" (pamphlet directory prepared by Christian Children's Fund, September 1991).

based. Not only do these offices provide CCF with a more visible presence in the international development arena; they also enable the agency to interact with these institutions, to learn from them and become aware of opportunities for collaboration.

CCF broke a "language barrier" in 1990 through the opening of a fundraising office in Paris. The next linguistic stop in the globalization of CCF's fundraising network will be Arabic. In McCleary's view the objective is not only to attract sponsors from the Muslim world, but also to launch CCF projects in the Middle East.

The foundation for a globally-oriented ecumenism was laid in the 1970s under Verent Mills, when CCF began to hire local people as "field representatives" in CCF's various overseas field offices. McCleary took another important symbolic step forward in this process by changing the title of field representative to national director.

CCF will do more than give credit to the national directors. It also seeks to learn from them and to integrate their perspective, priorities and expertise into the decisions that are made at headquarters in Richmond. To do this, McCleary has instituted a "Director in Residence" program, under which two or three national directors a year each spend several months in the Richmond office. "We bring in people from the Third World to participate in the decision-making process to help ensure that our decisions are more finely tuned to local Third World needs than to what we in Richmond might believe the needs to be," says McCleary.

In addition, some former national directors have come to Richmond to take on permanent positions: Joyce Dougan, former national director in Sierra Leone, became regional coordinator for Africa in 1990. Cora Espiritu, former national director in the Philippines, replaced David Herrell as director of program. Gonzalo Delgado, former national director in Bolivia, joined the ChildAlert office to work specifically on programs for street children before taking a position outside CCF.

~~~

It was during a visit of several national directors to Richmond, early in 1992, that a group of them had an opportunity to discuss their involvement with CCF, their hopes and dreams for their own countries, and their aspirations for the impact they might have personally on the lives of needy children. Included in the group were James Anywar-Ameda of Uganda, an agricultural economist, who at age 43 had just joined CCF; Abdou Mbacke of Senegal, a graduate in social work and a veteran of seven years with CCF; Adolfo E. Peters of Bolivia, with a Ph.D. in international development and economics, who had just joined CCF after years of college teaching and research; Norma S. de Sierra of Honduras, with CCF for almost a decade, who brought a background of law and planning to her CCF national office; and Tomasz Stachurski of Poland, a newspaper reporter, who had come to CCF in 1990. After ten days of intensive training and discussions at CCF headquarters, these five came together over lunch to assess their experiences just prior to heading back to their respective countries.

Their cultural differences were apparent as they dealt with an American restaurant accustomed to serving local folk. Adolfo Peters ordered a soft drink, Slice, "And, please, without ice!" he said. Abdou Mbacke followed suit, "A Coke, and, please, without ice!" Tomasz Stachurski's turn was next. In line with the his comrades, he gave his order in a thick and husky Polish voice, "Hot tea, and, please, without ice!" With this jovial cue, the group then ordered food. Each took great pains to make clear to the waiter just how his or her food was to be prepared, especially the meat. Abdou wanted his steak "well done" and he proceeded to send it back to the kitchen three times until the chef came personally to the table to ascertain directly if he truly wanted the piece of meat turned into a black char. He did, indeed, and finally got his steak "the way we like it in Africa," he said, poking fun at the American preference for bloody meat.

However different the group of five might be when it came to their palates, they were of a single mind in their desires to help children in their own countries and in the role they feel CCF should play toward that end. Aldolfo Peters described CCF as a "born baby" (i.e., it is alive and healthy) in Bolivia, directly assisting 16,000 children and through them a total of 100,000 people. In Bolivia families are large, accounting for the ratio of 16 to 100 between children assisted and those affected. When CCF helps just one child, the ripple effect is very large. But due to the decline of the mining business in Bolivia, CCF projects are focusing on agricultural development whose potential is unlimited there.

Asked why they are involved with CCF, they responded with amazing uniformity. Tomasz Stachurski was outspoken. CCF offers a new way of helping the community environment in Poland. Through CCF he hopes to help both Poland and the Polish people. His country needs new ideas about how to get communities and families moving. CCF's approach to things is excitiing indeed.

Abdou Mbacke said it is very easy to believe in CCF's mission. Everybody else in the international field seems to have some ulterior motive. But CCF is there solely to help children and their families.

Norma de Sierra thinks CCF offers one of the few real opportunities to help people. One can see concrete results from CCF's projects and programs, whereas most organizations only talk about making a difference. As a planner, she spent years talking about what ought to be done. But CCF offers one of the few opportunities of doing just that in the lives of the people of Honduras.

James Anywar-Ameda said that CCF's commitment to its mission is very appealing. This is a good way to make a difference in African society. Most other plans he has seen, only promise change. CCF, on the other hand, demonstrates change. Other organizations appear to be stuck in planning. Indeed, they do not seem to know how to move from planning to action.

Adolfo Peters thinks CCF offers one of the few ways of testing theories. He taught in the university for 17 years telling students what they must do to counter the problems of Bolivia. Now he is in a position where not only can he talk about what ought to be done, he can actually test what resulted from doing what he always taught. CCF, in essence, offers one of the few opportunities in the Western world to do something totally practical for children and families.

Tomasz Stachurski said that Poland will benefit greatly from CCF. Polish leaders have been searching for years for programs that directly assist people. CCF offers one of the few programs that can make a difference. Although CCF just moved into Poland during 1990, he sees the need as so great that he would like to be tied to CCF for years to come. CCF can touch the lives of Polish families on many different levels. Too many programs merely promise Polish people dollars. CCF, on the other hand, offers both dollars and help. And the help comes from the heart. It is a form of sharing with individuals and communities in other nations.

Abdou Mbacke remained rather quiet through most of the discussion. His steak finally cooked in the manner he wanted, he suddenly opened up. "Look, CCF is perceived at many different levels in all of these countries. There is first the target group—the people who are signed up in projects. The children get help and their families get help and their community is improved. But then there is the national level. When CCF speaks, it is important in our countries. The national government must listen, because CCF is there to help. Not to listen would be foolish. And then there is the third level," he continued. "CCF contributes to the economy of each of these countries. Grants, operating money, a national office and a staff—these are all important in countries where there are few national offices outside the government."

With great passion Abdou Mbacke finished his sermon. "CCF contributes to the national wealth, to agriculture, to health, to business. But it also does something else. It contributes directly to world peace. It is for all countries, all races, all traditions. All of these come together in CCF and we go back to our countries to help for peace. We have to do this! We must do this because, after all, the world is just one planetary village."

Nothing else needed to be said. The five national directors nodded in agreement as they completed a final repast before leaving Richmond for their various corners of the planetary village.

~~~

In December 1990, concern about the growing number of street children throughout the world caused Paul McCleary—today's devoted J. Calvett Clarke or Verent Mills of CCF—to visit a group of boys in Fortaleza, Brazil. McCleary sat with Cristiano, Francimar, Jose Walter and others in the small concrete courtyard of their beloved project building and talked about their plans for the future. McCleary challenged them and took them a step further than their dreams of becoming a policeman, a football player, or even a doctor or an engineer. When he asked the boys which of them would like to be President of Brazil, every hand shot up.

"I said, 'Okay, so if you were President, what would you do?'"

"I'd see that everybody had drinking water," said one boy.

"I'd make sure every family had a house," said another.

"I'd do away with poverty," said a third.

"Every family ought to have enough to eat," added a fourth boy.

"I thought to myself, this is disinterested vision," McCleary reflected later. "They're not talking about personal gain or honor, they're talking about what they would do for others to make this a different world. I couldn't help wondering, does CCF contribute to their ability to dream that they could be doctors or engineers? And, more importantly, would they have that disinterested concern for the world if it were not for CCF?"

As Paul McCleary sat in the brilliant Brazilian sunshine in that circle of young boys, he told them about a meeting he had attended in New York three months before: the World Summit for Children. Seventy-one heads of state met there together to ratify the United Nations Convention on the Rights of the Child. He told the boys that they are not dreaming alone. They, and the national leaders, and all the rest of us must see to it that the world keeps the promise it has made to its children. He told the boys that, together, we can realize their dream.

"We have a promise to keep," says McCleary. "We have made it possible for these children to dream of a different world, and we can't allow them to be disillusioned. We have to help them make the vision we have given them a reality."

A CHRONOLOGICAL
HISTORY OF CHRISTIAN
CHILDREN'S FUND

1887, June 30   J. Calvitt Clarke born in Brooklyn, New York (d. 1970), descended from a family once prominent in Mississippi and Louisiana. Involved with the YMCA as a child. A school dropout at age 14. Works successively for a publisher, the Presbyterian Mission Board, and Mt. Hermon School for Boys at Northfield, Massachusetts. Attends Denison University, Granville, Ohio. Receives M.A. from Washington and Jefferson College, Washington, Pennsylvania.

1913, Dec. 8   Clarke marries Helen Caroline Mattson (1894-1967), native of Irwin, Pennsylvania; after the marriage Mrs. Clarke, who becomes a virtual co-founder and co-director of CCF, continues her education at the University of Pittsburgh.

1918, April   Clarke graduates from Western Theological Seminary, Pittsburgh, and sails to Europe on a YMCA mission to assist displaced Russians in eastern Europe.

1919   Clarke joins Near East Relief (until 1931) and locates in Harrisburg, Pennsylvania, where he raises funds and collects goods and clothing for distressed peoples in the Middle East.

1924   Clarke visits Armenia for Near East Relief and witnesses starving children. He soon becomes Regional Director for southern U.S. and relocates to Richmond, Virginia (1927).

1931   Clarke becomes National Secretary of the Golden Rule
                Foundation and contributes volunteer efforts to the
                National Foundation for the Blind; Rev. Verent J. Mills
                (1913-), third Executive Director of CCF (1970-1981),
                begins his first missionary assignment in China.

1932   Clarke, Dr. J. Stewart Nagle, and Dr. John Voris co-
                found Save the Children Federation, Clarke serving as
                Southern Director from 1934 to 1937.

1937   Sino-Japanese War begins in Asia as Japan invades
                China, displacing millions of families and children.

1938, Aug.   Clarke and Dr. Nagle meet by chance in Chambersburg,
                Pennsylvania, where they discuss conditions in China
                and where Clarke is inspired to create a new relief
                fund for China's children.

CHINA'S CHILDREN FUND, 1938-1951

1938, Oct. 6   "China's Children Fund, Incorporated" is chartered
                by the State Corporation Commission of Virginia.

1938, Dec. 9   First meeting of China's Children Fund convened at
                12:30 p.m. in "a private dining room at the Occidental
                Restaurant, 212 N. Eighth St., Richmond, Va." Offic-
                ers elected: President, Eudora Ramsay Richardson;
                Secretary, T. Nelson Parker; Executive Secretary, J.
                Calvitt Clarke. Clarke's salary set at $50 per week
                commencing January 15, 1939. Offices opened in
                Richmond Trust Building on Main Street in Richmond.

1939, Feb. 21   Clarke reports 450 members of CCF's initial "National
                Committee" and the Board votes to send its first
                contribution, $2,000, immediately, "to the authorities
                in China."

1939, Dec. 27   Clarke reports more than $13,000 in contributions sent
                to KuKong Orphanage and to Ling Nan University in
                China.

1940, April 16 CCF makes first contribution directly to Madame

1940, Aug. 21	Chiang Kai-shek "for the children she is caring for." Judge Thomas W. Ozlin becomes Honorary Chairman of CCF. First contribution ($1,000) made to the National Child Welfare Association of China, a consortium of private relief funds.
1941, July 31	CCF's first "Adoption" Plan for Sponsors established with an initial subscription fee of $24 per year per child "adopted."
1941, Dec. 9	License issued to CCF by the U.S. government permitting money to be sent directly to China. With annual income of $169,712, CCF is assisting children in 29 orphanages.
1942, Jan. 9	Helen Clarke appointed assistant to the Executive Director at a salary of $20 per week.
1942, May 27	CCF Board invites "a Hebrew" to serve on its Executive Committee.
1942, June	Verent Mills leads escape of 142 children from Toishan, China, and the invading Japanese army over a distance of more than 300 miles to Dr. J. R. Saunders' CCF-assisted orphanage in KuKong.
1942, Aug. 6	Dr. J. R. Saunders of KuKong Orphanage designated "our representative in China."
1942, Dec. 29	After much deliberation, CCF declines participation in the United China Relief Program of the U.S. government's War Relief Control Board.
1943, June 18	CCF reluctantly joins the United China Relief Program, fearing the loss of its ability to raise funds privately.
1943, Nov. 26	Erwin W. Raetz is appointed to coordinate CCF's China operations.
1944, Oct. 10	CCF withdraws in protest from the United China Relief Program.

1944, Nov. 8	Mrs. Richardson resigns from presidency of CCF; T. Nelson Parker becomes new President; Verbon Kemp, later Executive Director of CCF, is elected to the Executive Committee. Total funds raised for the year $263,923, assisting 45 orphanages in China.
1945, Aug.	Verent Mills moves 700 children from Toishan to Canton with aid from General Cheung Fat Foi; in Canton he meets Erwin Raetz and asks CCF to assist his orphanage.
1946, Feb. 7	CCF Board votes to expand operations into the Philippines and on May 10 to assist a project in Burma.
1946, June-July	Clarke travels to China, visiting 21 orphanages while there; Verent Mills travels to Canton to meet Clarke.
1947, Spring	Rev. Erwin Raetz appointed head of CCF Far Eastern Office in Hong Kong; Verent Mills shortly thereafter is appointed Overseas Director and is placed in Shanghai to expand into North China, Korea, and Japan; CCF soon begins assisting existing orphanages in other nations including Malaysia, Indonesia, Borneo, and India—famous Alwaye School and Settlement in Kerala State of India, founded by British missionaries in 1927, taken over by CCF; other initiatives are begun in Italy and Germany following World War II.
1948, Fall	CCF establishes a Korean Committee chaired by Mrs. Ethel Underwood, wife of CCF treasurer Dr. Horace Underwood; Verent Mills sent to Korea and signs up five existing orphanages to be assisted by CCF; from Korea he proceeds to Japan, signing up additional orphanages.
1949	Japanese government asks CCF to establish a training college for social welfare workers; Izumi College is built next to CCF's Bott Memorial Home and operated by CCF.
1949, Jan.-Feb.	Communist revolt begins in South Korea, threatening destabilization of government.

1949, March 17   Ethel Underwood is assassinated by Communist guerrillas in the Underwood home in Seoul, Korea, just after she opened the Seoul Home for Girls; nevertheless, 5 additional Korean homes opened by summer.

1949, Oct. 1   Communist government established on mainland China; Verent Mills visits orphanages in China one month later and finds homes and children in good condition.

1950   Rev. Verent Mills departs from mainland China escaping the Communist government and is appointed Overseas Director for CCF (1951) as Rev. Erwin Raetz resigns; establishes a headquarters in Hong Kong; initiatives to assist orphanages in Lebanon, Syria, and Palestine begin. During the year CCF moves from rented quarters to three town houses nearby at 106, 108, and 110 South Third Street, purchased and converted to its needs.

1950, June 25   North Korea invades South Korea, displacing millions of people.

1950, June   Battle for control of central Korea begins; China joins the war in support of North Korea; by the end of the year UN forces are driven from Seoul to the South; two million Koreans are killed and other millions made homeless.

1950, Oct. 1   CCF discontinues assistance to orphanages in China, giving up 46 orphanages, $1-2 million in property, and 5,113 children; new centers are opened in Hong Kong, Macao, and Taiwan to care for transferees and refugees.

1950, Dec.   Colonel Dean Hess of the U.S. Fifth Air Force and former pastor from Marietta, Ohio, organizes plane rescue of CCF orphans from Seoul to Cheju Island inspiring the movie *Battle Hymn*; Verent Mills receives the children and creates a large home at a former Japanese agricultural college.

FROM CHINA TO THE WORLD, 1951-1963

1951, Feb. 6	Official name of CCF changed from China's Children Fund to Christian Children's Fund, recognizing the growing worldwide focus of CCF.
1951, June	CCF orphanages in Korea increase from 5 to 17 in one year as the expanding war in central Korea makes more than 10 million people homeless.
1953, July 27	Armistice is signed in Korea where CCF owns 23 orphanages serving more than 4,000 children; Dr. Roe Chin Pak, a Korean, is appointed to head CF's Korean program—the first indigenous national director; assistance to American Indian tribes begun; shortly thereafter, assistance to Latin America launched.
1955	CCF's expansion throughout Asia has reached 15 Asian nations and hundreds of orphanages.
1956, Fall	Universal-International Pictures releases the film *Battle Hymn* based on 1951 rescue of Korean CCF children by Colonel Dean Hess.
1957	Publication of John C. Caldwell's *Children of Calamity* (New York: John Day Company), a dramatic description of CCF's work around the world resulting from Caldwell's visits to CCF projects in 15 countries.
1957, Spring	Dr. and Mrs. Clarke received by Emperor and Empress of Japan in the Royal Palace; in Hong Kong CCF opens "Children's Garden," a special dream of Mrs. Clarke. The largest cottage-plan orphanage in the Far East, with 65 cottages housing more than 1,000 children, this was the culmination of CCF's direct property acquisition and development.
1958	CCF assists 38,000 children in 72 orphanages in Korea—its peak of using this form of assistance; Clarke awarded Ribbon of Honor by President Syngman Rhee in Seoul, Korea; Dr. and Mrs. Clarke received by Madame Chiang Kai-shek at Presidential Residence in Taiwan; Verent Mills, Overseas Director located in

Hong Kong, is transferred to CCF headquarters in Richmond.

1960   The Korean Association of Voluntary Agencies (KAVA) reports that CCF's orphanage program may encourage some families to abandon children for the superb care and education CCF provides; CCF responds by developing its unique "Family Helper Program" and expanding it quickly to Taiwan and Brazil.

1960   Christian Children's Fund of Canada formed as the first affiliated national program outside the United States.

1960, Spring   Clarke Junior College—devoted to training individuals in social work, child welfare, and related disciplines—is dedicated in Japan with Dr. and Mrs. Clarke in attendance; by now CCF is assisting 36,000 children around the world with annual gifts from more than 100,000 individuals.

1961, March 13   Clarke installed by Japanese Emperor in the Order of the Sacred Teasure at Japanese Consulate in New York.

1961, October   Publication of *Yankee Si! The Story of Dr. J. Calvitt Clarke and His 36,000 Children* (New York: William Morrow & Company) written by Edmund W. Janss and based on his visits to more than one hundred CCF projects; Janss reports that CCF assists 36,000 children in 50 countries at 429 projects (including 93 in Korea, 60 in Japan, and 17 in Hong Kong).

1962   Clarke presented China's Order of the Brilliant Star at Presidential Residence in Taiwan; also presented Order of Cultural Merit from South Korea.

1963, Dec. 10   Dr. and Mrs. Clarke, due to their advancing ages and with encouragement from the Board of Directors, submit their resignations; Verbon E. Kemp (1900-1981), Executive Director of the Virginia State Chamber of Commerce, replaces Clarke as the second Executive Director of CCF (1964-1970); Clarke is desig-

153

nated as Executive Director Emeritus; feeling too inactive in the resulting organization, the Clarkes join their daughter, Jeanne, in 1964 to form a new sponsorship agency, Children, Incorporated.

FROM ORPHANAGE TO FAMILY ASSISTANCE, 1963-1974

1964 — South American program begun with a "family helper" approach to assistance projects.

1965, July — CCF moves into new headquarters building at 203 East Cary Street in Richmond, constructed with the use of bequests and other non-sponsorship funds; records of CCF are computerized for the first time.

1967 — CCF adopts two major systemwide policy changes: (1) national programs wherever possible are to be headed by nationals and (2) "family helper" approach supplants assistance for children in orphanages as principal program thrust; CCF is in 56 countries assisting 75,000 children in more than 700 projects.

1970 — Verbon Kemp retires and is replaced by Verent J. Mills (1913-) as CCF's third Executive Director (1970-1981).

1971 — CCF is assisting 133,555 children of whom 88,455 are in orphanages or boarding schools.

1972 — Mills commissions full-fledged evaluation of CCF's philosophy and practices by Dr. Charles G. Chakerian, social scientist from the University of Chicago; another audit conducted five years later by Dr. Ahti Hailuoto of the International Union for Child Welfare, Geneva, Switzerland; the audits lead to expansion of Family Helper programs (Chakerian) and creation of community development programs (Hailuoto); CCF's focus shifts from orphanages and boarding schools to community-based projects.

1972 — CCF-Boernefonden, Christian Children's Fund of Denmark, formed, the second national CCF affiliate.

1973   CCF opens an African office in Nairobi, Kenya; soon CCF leaves Europe and the Middle East to permit greater concentration on Africa.

1974   Japan's CCF program after 26 years becomes independent and self-supporting with the creation of the Christian Child Welfare Association of Japan (CCWA).

FROM CHARITY TO COMMUNITY DEVELOPMENT, 1974-1988

1974, Sept.   General Accounting Office issues report on *Children's Charities, 1974*, critical of five children's organizations including Christian Children's Fund.

1974, Oct. 1   Columnist Jack Anderson issues a stormy column on CCF making use of part of the GAO report focusing on the use of funds by third party institutions receiving assistance from CCF.

1974, Oct. 10   Senator Walter Mondale convenes subcommittee hearings on "Voluntary Foreign Aid Agencies Serving Children and Youth"; Verent Mills appears for CCF, citing changes that will be made in CCF policies.

1976, Sept. 8   CCF adopts a strict "Code of Fundraising Ethics."

1976   Television actress Sally Struthers becomes honorary National Chairman and public spokesperson for CCF; soon television and magazine ads featuring Struthers begin to appear.

1977   Hong Kong's CCF program becomes self-supporting with the creation of The Hongkong Children & Youth Services.

1978   CCF third national affiliate, CCF Kinderhilfswerk e.V., founded in Germany.

1981, July   Verent Mills retires and James MacCracken (1922-), Vice President for Program of Save the Children Federation, is selected to become the fourth Executive Director of CCF (until 1988).

1983	CCF's fourth national affiliate, Christian Children's Fund of Great Britain, formed.
1983, June 30	In an 18-month special promotional program ending on this date, MacCracken successfully challenged CCF organization to increase the number of assisted children from 260,000 to 325,000.
1985	Chinese Children's Fund formed to take over CCF operations in Taiwan; Christian Children's Fund of Australia also formed.
1986	Dr. Chun Wai Chan of Fresno, California, former CCF child at Faith Love Home in Hong Kong from 1959 to 1967, becomes first former CCF-sponsored child to be elected to CCF's Board of Directors; Korea Children's Foundation formed.
1987	CCF presented a Presidential End Hunger Award by the U.S. Agency for International Development.
1988, Oct. 21	James MacCracken retires and Paul McCleary (1930-) becomes the fifth Executive Director of CCF (1988-present).

A GLOBAL FORCE FOR ACTION, 1988 AND BEYOND

1989, April	CCF national affiliates convene in Richmond to consider the formation of a World Alliance of CCFs.
1989, Oct.	CCF visited by delegation from Minsk, USSR, concerning children afflicted by the 1986 Chernobyl nuclear power plant disaster.
1989, Nov. 20	UN General Assembly adopts the Convention on the Rights of the Child, CCF represented by Honorary Chair Sally Struthers, Chairman Dr. R. Jackson Sadler, and Paul McCleary.
1990, Jan.	CCF establishes "ChildAlert," an emergency intervention and assistance program, to help children caught in especially difficult circumstances.

1990	Sally Struthers receives a Presidential End Hunger Award for her work in promoting CCF and world-wide child welfare awareness; Christian Children's Fund of New Zealand is formed in Auckland and Un Enfant Par La Main is organized in Paris, France.
1990, July	CCF national office is opened in Warsaw, Poland, marking the reentry of CCF into Europe.
1990, Sept. 4	Convention on the Rights of the Child ratified by the necessary 20 nations, enters into force as international law.
1990, Sept. 29-30	Seventy-one heads of state and other delegates attend a World Summit for Children in New York City and adopt a Declaration and Plan of Action to implement the new Convention; Paul McCleary attends both as Executive Director of CCF and as an officer of the NGO Committee to UNICEF.
1990, Nov. 1	World Alliance of Christian Children's Funds formed, uniting CCF with the other national Funds it has created in Australia, Canada, Denmark, Germany, Great Britain, Hong Kong, Japan, Korea, and Taiwan.
1991, Jan. 20	McCleary announces policy commitment, "Ten Steps to 2000," CCF's plan for implementing the Declaration of the World Summit, at CCF's Latin America Regional Conference.
1991, May 10	CCF moves from 203 East Cary Street to new offices in Richmond suburbs at 2821 Emerywood Parkway.
1991, May 30	Her Majesty Queen Noor of Jordan is the first head of state to visit CCF's new international headquarters.
1991, July 15	CCF's new facilities officially inaugurated with the presence of Congressman Thomas J. Bliley, Jr., of Virginia; Senora Telma Pinto de Espina Salguero, the Second Lady of Guatemala; and delegations from Canada, Latvia, and Belorussia.

PRESIDENTS OF THE BOARD OF DIRECTORS
CHRISTIAN CHILDREN'S FUND, 1938-1992

1938-1944	Mrs. Eudora Ramsay Richardson
1944-1973	T. Nelson Parker
1973	John J. Fairbank, Jr. (completing Parker's unexpired term)
1973-1976	W. Stirling King
1976-1979	Lee F. Davis
1979-1984	Dr. Thomas W. Murrell, Jr.
1984-1987	C. Hobson Goddin
1987-1989	Landon W. Trigg
1989-1992	Dr. R. Jackson Sadler

APPENDIX 1

ANNUAL REVENUES AND AMOUNTS PROVIDED TO
PROGRAMS BY CHRISTIAN CHILDREN'S FUND, 1938-1991

Year	Receipts	Provided to Programs
1938-39	$ 10,344	$ 2,700
1939-40	35,279	10,000
1940-41	95,900	43,000
1941-42	169,712	134,555
1942-43	168,183	135,000
1943-44	263,923	186,726
1944-45	263,291	128,607
1945-46	334,165	372,217
1946-47	424,535	349,589
1947-48	477,434	446,182
1948-49	525,119	494,203
1949-50	524,996	414,640
1950-51	462,537	279,464
1951-52	620,701	463,323
1952-53	958,251	697,797
1953-54	1,391,276	972,926
1954-55	1,430,091	1,011,314
1955-56	1,953,975	1,940,650
1956-57	3,577,755	2,619,707
1957-58	3,941,172	2,977,535
1958-59	4,203,420	3,119,795
1959-60	4,583,939	3,515,472

1960-61	3,973,621	2,741,729
1961-62	4,367,245	3,070,133
1962-63	4,732,878	3,378,189
1963-64	5,358,689	3,801,142
1964-65	6,042,862	4,701,649
1965-66	6,645,507	5,075,661
1966-67	6,387,128	4,265,990
1967-68	10,155,562	6,343,442
1968-69	13,327,283	9,455,631
1969-70	15,429,026	11,881,219
1970-71	17,726,736	13,289,811
1971-72	20,849,226	16,584,018
1972-73	24,890,461	20,672,380
1973-74	28,665,413	23,359,710
1974-75	28,842,015	23,403,034
1975-76	27,971,370	22,257,352
1976-77	29,234,888	23,854,976
1977-78	31,306,879	25,471,643
1978-79	34,658,479	27,862,157
1979-80	37,528,161	30,254,934
1980-81	42,054,264	33,995,830
1981-82	47,381,854	38,008,161
1982-83	58,167,745	47,076,767
1983-84	64,603,855	51,856,857
1984-85	74,310,911	59,604,387
1985-86	81,247,444	65,923,097
1986-87	85,061,502	67,878,026
1987-88	92,712,085	74,376,604
1988-89	101,743,506	75,883,769
1989-90	102,952,735	79,323,409
1990-91	102,959,701	82,556,010
1991-92	106,094,588	84,201,860
TOTALS	$1,349,799,617	$1,062,724,979

APPENDIX 2

NATIONS WHERE CHRISTIAN CHILDREN'S FUND HAS
SPONSORED LONG-TERM PROJECTS, 1938-1992

Antigua-Barbuda
Argentina
Austria
Bangladesh
Belgium
Bolivia
Brazil
Burundi
Cameroon
Canada
Chile
China
Colombia
Costa Rica
Dominica
Dominican Republic
Ecuador
Egypt
El Salvador
England
Estonia
Ethiopia
Finland
France
The Gambia
Germany
Greece
Guatemala

Haiti
Honduras
Hong Kong
India
Indonesia
Iran
Israel
Italy
Jamaica
Japan
Jordan
Kenya
Korea
Latvia
Lebanon
Lithuania
Macao
Malaysia
Mexico
Montserrat
Myanmar
Nicaragua
Niger
Nigeria
Okinawa
Pakistan
Paraguay
Poland

The Philippines
Portugal
Puerto Rico
Rwanda
St. Kitts-Nevis
St. Vincent and the
    Grenadines
Scotland
Senegal
Sierra Leone
Singapore
South Africa
Spain
Sri Lanka
Swaziland
Switzerland
Syria
Taiwan
Thailand
Togo
Turkey
Uganda
United States
Uruguay
Vietnam
Zambia
Zimbabwe

APPENDIX 3

CHRISTIAN CHILDREN'S FUND
AROUND THE WORLD, 1992

<u>World Alliance Member Organizations</u>

Christian Children's Fund, Inc.
Richmond, Virginia, U.S.A.
Dr. Paul F. McCleary, Executive Director

Christian Children's Fund of Australia
Sydney, Australia
Robert A. Brooks, National Director

Christian Children's Fund of Canada
Scarborough, Ontario, Canada
Peter Harris, National Director

BOERNEfonden
Copenhagen, Denmark
Soeren Stenum, National Director

CCF Kinderhilfswerk e.V.
Nuertingen, Germany
Conny Wolf, National Director

Christian Children's Fund of Great Britain
London, England
Robert J. H. Edwards, National Director

The Hongkong Children & Youth Services
Kowloon, Hong Kong
Mary-L. Beyns, Agency Director

Christian Child Welfare Association of Japan (CCWA)
Tokyo, Japan
Takeshi Kobayashi, National Director

Korea Children's Foundation, Inc.
Seoul, Korea
Dr. Youn Keun Cha, National Director

Chinese Children's Fund
Taichung, Taiwan
Charles Tung-Yau Kuo, National Director

International Partnership Organizations

France: Un Enfant Par La Main
Candice Nancel, National Director

New Zealand: Christian Children's Fund of New Zealand
Jill Eagle, Manager

National Offices

Antigua, St. John's
Allison Y. Barnes, National Director

Bolivia, La Paz
Dr. Adolfo E. Peters, National Director

Brazil, Belo Horizonte
Ely Domingues Gomes, National Director

Brazil, Fortaleza
Vera Alves de Lima, National Director

Colombia, Bogota
Eugenia Franco O., National Director

Ecuador, Quito
Galo Pozo A., National Director

Ethiopia, Addis Ababa
Ketema Abebe, National Director

The Gambia, Banjul
Pa-Louis Furmose Gomez, National Director

Guatemala, Guatemala City
Dr. Luis Rolando Torres C., National Director

Haiti, Port-au-Prince
Cecile Gaboton, National Director

Honduras, Tegucigalpa
Norma S. de Sierra, National Director

India, Bangalore
Christopher S. Gojer, National Director

India, New Delhi
Naval K. Dave, National Director

Indonesia, Jakarta
Bernardine Wirjana, National Director

Kenya, Nairobi
Margery Kabuya, National Director

Mexico, Mexico City
Cristina Casares, National Director

Philippines, Manila
Maria Saturnina L. Hamili, National Director

Poland, Warsaw
Tomasz Stachurski, National Director

Senegal, Dakar
Abdou Mbacke, National Director

Sierra Leone, Freetown
Dr. Joseph Conteh, National Director

Sri Lanka, Colombo
S.B.R. Nikahetiya, National Director

Thailand, Bangkok
Amporn Wathanavongs, National Director

Togo, Lome
Egbemimo Houmey, National Director

Uganda, Kampala
Charles James Anywar-Ameda, National Director

Zambia, Lusaka
Silverio L. Chimuka, National Director

International Partner Agencies

Estonian Central Union for Child Welfare
Estonia, Tallinn
Dr. Leo Tamm, President

Latvia Children's Fund
Latvia, Riga
Andris Berzinch, President

Lithuania Children's Fund
Lithuania, Vilnius
Juozas Nekrosius, President

United States Program Offices

Virginia, Richmond
Tom Rhodenbaugh, Director of the U.S. Program

Mississippi, Jackson
Wendell Paris, Program Director

Montana, Great Falls
John Johnson, Area Program Coordinator

North Dakota, Bismark
Delinda McKay, Area Program Coordinator

Oklahoma, Park Hill
U.S. Sponsor Services Office

Vicki Buck, Sponsor Services Director
Charlie Soap, Program Director

South Dakota, Rapid City
Sheila Miller, Area Program Coordinator

South Dakota, Sioux Falls
Ferris Joseph, Area Program Coordinator

Texas, McAllen
Oscar Espinoza, Director

Liaison Offices

California, Los Angeles
Pam Sharp, CCF Representative

New York, New York
Carol Smolenski, CCF Representative

Romania, Bucharest
Valerie Ciofu, CCF Representative

Switzerland, Geneva
Dr. Eugene Ries, Director, European Programs
Dr. Zdzislaw Pawlik, Director, Eastern and Central European Programs

Washington, D.C.
Arthur Simon, CCF Representative

INDEX

Please refer to the Chronological History of CCF included with this volume for additional details not necessarily included in this index.